HUMAN INTELLIGENCE

transaction book series

HUMAN INTELLIGENCE

Edited by
J. McVicker Hunt

*trans*action *books*
New Brunswick, New Jersey
Distributed by E. P. Dutton and Company

Unless otherwise indicated, the essays in this book originally appeared in *trans*action magazine

*trans*action *books*
Rutgers University
New Brunswick, New Jersey 08903

Library of Congress Catalog Card Number: 78-164977
ISBN: 0-87855-002-X (cloth); 0-87855-502-1 (paper)

Printed in the United States of America

Contents

Preface

For the past eight years, *trans*action magazine has dedicated itself to the task of reporting the strains and conflicts within the American system. But the magazine has done more than this. It has pioneered in social programs for changing the society, offered the kind of analysis that has permanently restructured the terms of the "dialogue" between peoples and publics, and offered the sort of prognosis that makes for real alterations in social and political policies directly affecting our lives.

The work done in the pages of *trans*action has crossed disciplinary boundaries. This represents much more than simple cross-disciplinary "team efforts." It embodies rather a recognition that the social world cannot be easily carved into neat academic disciplines; that, indeed, the study of the experience of blacks in American ghettos, or the manifold uses and abuses of agencies of law enforcement, or the sorts of overseas policies that lead to the celebration of some dictatorships and the condemnation of others, can best be examined from many viewpoints and from the vantage points of many disciplines.

Now the editors of *trans*action magazine are making available in permanent form the most important work done in the magazine, supplemented in some cases by additional materials edited to reflect the tone and style developed over the years by *trans*action. Like the magazine, this series of books demonstrates the superiority of starting with real world problems and searching out practical solutions, over the zealous guardianship of professional boundaries. Indeed, it is precisely this approach that has elicited enthusiastic support from leading American social scientists, many of whom are represented among the editors of these volumes.

The subject matter of these books concerns social changes and social policies that have aroused the long-standing needs and present-day anxieties of us all. These changes are in organizational lifestyles, concepts of human ability and intelligence, changing patterns of norms and morals, the relationship of social conditions to physical and biological environments, and in the status of social science with respect to national policy making. The editors feel that many of these articles have withstood the test of time, and match in durable interest the best of available social science literature. This collection of *trans*action articles, then, attempts to address itself to immediate issues without violating the basic insights derived from the classical literature in the various fields of social science.

As the crises of the sixties have given way to the economic crunch of the seventies, the social scientists involved as editors and authors of this series have gone beyond observation of critical areas, and have entered into the vital and difficult tasks of explanation and interpretation. They have defined issues in a way that makes solutions possible. They have provided answers as well as asked the right questions. These books, based as they are upon the best materials from *trans*action magazine, are dedicated not to the highlighting of social problems alone, but to establishing guidelines for social solutions based on the social sciences.

THE EDITORS
*trans*action

Introduction

J. MCVICKER HUNT

Few conceptions of the behavioral and social sciences have been undergoing more rapid change than that of intelligence and its role in human competence. Few conceptions of these sciences are more intimately intertwined with social policy as such policy influences social change for better or worse. In the eight years that *trans*action magazine has been dedicated, as the editors have put it, "to the task of reporting the strains and conflicts in the American system," it has published a number of articles which have illuminated various aspects of this highly important domain. Taken individually, each sheds its light over but a limited portion of the whole. Taken together, these vignettes illuminate and contribute significantly to dialogue; and in these ways they influence social policy decisions regarding early childhood education and various aspects of education which foster or hamper the development of

1

competence and its utilization in society. The impact of these essays becomes more significant as they are brought together in a single book.

The essays comprising this anthology fall roughly into the four categories indicated in the table of contents. Part I, comprised of three subsections, is concerned with whether the heritability indices of intelligence test performance have anything to say about the educability of individuals, with the implications of plasticity in psychological development and the role of experience in the development of competence, and with the two kinds of intelligence. Part II concerns various aspects of social class and education in the development of competence. Part III is concerned with the differences between and similarities of creativity and intelligence. Part IV contains suggestions for improving the status quo. One is concerned with improving the treatment of the retarded, another with using techniques of reinforcement to change the climate of the classroom, a third suggests an improvement on the practice of tracking in high schools, and the final one makes a plea for criteria of hiring which are more relevant to competence on the job.

This anthology should be of interest to a wide variety of people. It could well serve as a readable introduction to the changing conceptions of intelligence for laymen generally and for those with political responsibility. It should be of interest to teachers. It could well serve as supplementary reading for courses in intelligence or intelligence testing, in child development, in educational psychology, and perhaps even in personnel selection and in labor relations.

Such anthologies have taken on new importance for both laymen and students in recent years. As they face moments of decision on social policies, many laymen find need to become informed through accurate but nontechnical presentations of the matters concerned. Seldom can they take the time for a library search or even a search through the issues of a magazine like *trans*action. For them, having the relevant articles assembled in an inexpensive book is a great time-saving boon. Anthologies have also acquired new importance in the colleges. Since World War II when the GIs returned to the campuses, the reserve desks at college libraries have become frustrating bottlenecks for students seeking the readings which have been assigned to supplement the textbooks. Again, inexpensive anthologies which supplement textbooks are a time-saving boon for students.

No claim of comprehensive coverage is made for this work, yet, taken together, the articles in this anthology will shed light on a great deal of the domain of human intelligence and competence and the factors which influence it. Moreover, the supplementary readings both extend the coverage and supply leads to the basic investigative literature which, if followed, can open the whole field in relatively rapid order.

BACKGROUND FACTORS

Part I.

Genetics and Competence: Do Heritability Indices Predict Educability?

JERRY HIRSCH

Over the past two decades the case against extreme behaviorism has been spelled out in incontrovertible detail. The behaviorists committed many sins: they accepted the mind at birth as Locke's *tabula rasa,* they advocated an empty-organism psychology, they asserted the uniformity postulate of no prenatal individual differences; in short, they epitomized typological thinking. Many times we have heard quoted the famous boast by the first high priest of behaviorism, John B. Watson:

Give me a dozen healthy infants, well-formed, and my own specified world to bring them up in, and I'll guarantee to take any one at random and train him to become any type of specialist I might select— doctor, lawyer, artist, merchant-chief and yes, even beggar-man and thief, regardless of his talents, penchants, tendencies, abilities, vocations, race of his ancestors.

7

However, it is only when we read the next sentence, which is rarely, if ever, quoted, that we begin to understand how so many people might have embraced something intellectually so shallow as radical behaviorism. In that all-important next sentence Watson explains: "I am going beyond my facts and I admit it, but so have the advocates of the contrary and they have been doing it for many thousands of years."

Who were the advocates of the contrary, and what had they been saying? It is difficult to establish the origins of racist thinking, but certainly one of its most influential advocates was Joseph Arthur de Gobineau, who published a four-volume *Essay on the Inequality of the Human Races* in the mid-1850s. De Gobineau preached the superiority of the white race, and among whites it was the Aryans who carried civilization to its highest point. In fact, they were responsible for civilization wherever it appeared. Unfortunately, de Gobineau's essay proved to be the major seminal work that inspired some of the most perverse developments in the intellectual and political history of our civilization. Later in his life, de Gobineau became an intimate of Richard Wagner. Houston Stewart Chamberlain, an Englishman who emigrated to the Continent, became a devoted admirer of both de Gobineau and Wagner. In 1908, after Wagner's death, Chamberlain married Wagner's daughter during World War I, becoming a naturalized German citizen in 1916.

In the summer of 1923, an admirer of Chamberlain's writings, Adolf Hitler, visited Wahnfried, the Wagner family home in Bayreuth where Chamberlain lived. After their meeting, Chamberlain wrote to Hitler: "My faith in the Germans had never wavered for a moment, but my hope . . . had sunk to a low ebb. At one stroke you have transformed the state of my soul!" We all know the sequel to that unfortunate tale. I find that many of my scientific colleagues, whether they be biological or social scientists, for the most part, do not know the sad parallel that exists for the essentially political tale I have so far recounted. The same theme can be traced down the mainstream of biosocial science.

Today not many people know the complete title of Darwin's most famous book: *On the Origin of Species by Means of Natural Selection or the Preservation of Favored Races in the Struggle for Life*. I find no evidence that Darwin had the attitudes we now call racist. Unfortunately, many of his admirers, his contemporaries and his successors were not as circumspect as he. In Paris in 1838, J.E.D. Esquirol first described a form of mental deficiency later to become well known by two inappropriate names unrelated to his work. Unhappily, one of these names, through textbook adoption and clinical jargon, puts into wide circulation a term loaded with race prejudice. Somewhat later (1846 and 1866), E. Seguin described the same condition under the name "furfuraceous cretinism," but his account has only recently been recognized as "the most ingenious description of physical characteristics," as C.E. Benda puts it.

This most promising scientific beginning was ignored, however, and in 1866, John Langdon Haydon Down published the paper entitled "Observations on an Ethnic Classification of Idiots."

. . .making a classification of the feeble-minded, by arranging them around various ethnic standards—in other words, framing a natural system to supplement the information to be derived by an inquiry into the history of the case.

I have been able to find among the large number
of idiots and imbeciles which comes under my
observation, both at Earlswood and the outpatient
department of the Hospital, that a considerable
portion can be fairly referred to one of the great
divisions of the human family other than the class
from which they have sprung. Of course, there are
numerous representatives of the great Caucasian
family. Several well-marked examples of the Ethio-
pian variety have come under my notice, presenting
the characteristic malar bones, the prominent eyes,
the puffy lips, and retreating chin. The woolly hair
has also been present, although not always black nor
has the skin acquired pigmentary deposit. They have
been specimens of white negroes, although of European descent.

Some arrange themselves around the Malay variety, and present in their soft, black, curly hair, their
prominent upper jaws and capacious mouths, types
of the family which people the South Sea Islands.

Nor have there been wanting the analogues of the
people who with shortened foreheads, prominent
cheeks, deep-set eyes, and slightly apish nose, originally inhabited the American Continent.

The great Mongolian family has numerous representatives, and it is to this division, I wish, in this
paper, to call special attention. A very large number
of congenital idiots are typical Mongols. So marked is
this, that when placed side by side, it is difficult to
believe that the specimens compared are not children
of the same parents. The number of idiots who
arrange themselves around the Mongolian type is so
great, and they present such a close resemblance to
one another in mental power, that I shall describe an

idiot member of this racial division, selected from the large number that have fallen under my observation.

The hair is not black, as in the real Mongol, but of a brownish colour, straight and scanty. The face is flat and broad, and destitute of prominence. The cheeks are roundish, and extended laterally. The eyes are obliquely placed, and the internal canthi more than normally distant from one another. The palpebral fissure is very narrow. The forehead is wrinkled transversely from the constant assistance which the levatores palpebrarum derive from the occipito-frontalis muscle in the opening of the eyes. The lips are large and thick with transverse fissures. The tongue is long, thick, and is much roughened. The nose is small. The skin has a slight dirty yellowish tinge and is deficient in elasticity, giving the appearance of being too large for the body.

The boy's aspect is such that it is difficult to realize that he is the child of Europeans, but so frequently are these characters presented, that there can be no doubt that these ethnic features are the result of degeneration.

And he means degeneration from a higher to a lower race. The foregoing represents a distasteful but excellent example of the racial hierarchy theory and its misleadingly dangerous implications. That was how the widely used terms "mongolism" and "mongolian idiocy" entered our "technical" vocabulary. For the next century, this pattern of thought would persist and occupy an important place in the minds of many leading scientists.

In 1884, Francis Galton, Darwin's half cousin, founder of the eugenics movement and respected contributor to many fields of science, wrote to the distinguished Swiss botanist Alphonse de Candolle: "It strikes me that

the Jews are specialized for a parasitical existence upon
other nations, and that there is need of evidence that
they are capable of fulfilling the varied duties of a
civilized nation by themselves." Karl Pearson, Galton's
disciple and biographer, echoed this opinion 40 years
later during his attempt to prove the undesirability of
Jewish immigration into Britain: "for such men as
religion, social habits, or language keep as a caste apart,
there should be no place. They will not be absorbed by,
and at the same time strengthen the existing population;
they will develop into a parasitic race."

Beginning in 1908 and continuing at least until 1928,
Karl Pearson collected and analyzed data in order to
assess "the quality of the racial stock immigrating into
Great Britain." He was particularly disturbed by the
large numbers of East European Jews, who near the turn
of the century began coming from Poland and Russia to
escape the pogroms. Pearson's philosophy was quite
explicitly spelled out:

> Let us admit . . . .that the mind of man is for the
> most part a congenital product, and the factors
> which determine it are racial and familial; we are not
> dealing with a mutable characteristic capable of being
> moulded by the doctor, the teacher, the parent or
> the home environment . . . .The ancestors of the men
> who pride themselves on being English today were all
> at one time immigrants; it is not for us to cast the
> first stone against newcomers, solely because they are
> newcomers. But the test for immigrants in the old
> days was a severe one; it was power physical and
> mental to retain their hold on the land they seized.
> So came Celts, Saxons, Norsemen, Danes and Nor-
> mans in succession and built up the nation of which
> we are proud. Nor do we criticize the alien Jewish

immigration simply because it is Jewish; we took the
alien Jews to study, because they were the chief
immigrants of that day and material was readily
available.

His observations led him to conclude: "Taken *on the
average,* and regarding both sexes this alien Jewish
population is somewhat inferior physically and mentally
to the native population." Pearson proclaimed this
general Jewish inferiority despite his own failure to find
any differences between the Jewish and non-Jewish
boys when comparisons (reported in the same article)
were made for the sexes separately.

Quite recently there has appeared a series of papers
disputing whether or not black Americans are, in fact,
genetically inferior to white Americans in intellectual
capacity. In 1969 a discussion of heredity, race and
intelligence reasserting the old fallacious white suprema-
cist point of view was published in the *Harvard
Educational Review* by the notorious A.R. Jensen of the
University of California at Berkeley. The claims and
counterclaims have been given enormous publicity in
the popular press in America. Some of those papers
contain most of the fallacies that can conceivably be
associated with this widely misunderstood problem.

This dispute leads to an intellectual cul-de-sac, and a
series of steps marked by fallacious assumptions that
can be listed as follows: 1) a trait called intelligence is
defined, and an instrument for measuring the expression
of this trait is devised and used; 2) the heritability of the
trait is estimated; 3) races (populations) are compared
with respect to their performance on the test of trait
expression; 4) when the races (populations) differ on
the test whose heritability has now been measured, the
one with the lower score is genetically inferior, Q.E.D.

The foregoing argument can be applied to any single trait or to as many traits as one might choose to consider. Therefore, analysis of this general problem does *not* depend upon the particular definition and test used for this or that trait. For my analysis I shall pretend that an acceptable test exists for some trait, be it height, weight, intelligence or anything else. For without an acceptable test, discussion of the "trait" remains unscientific.

In order even to consider comparisons between races, the following concepts must be recognized: 1) the mosaic nature of the genome or hereditary endowment of the species; 2) development as the expression of one out of many alternatives in the norm of reaction (see below) of the genotype or hereditary endowment of the individual; 3) a population as a gene pool or reservoir of possible genetic combinations; 4) heritability (a measure of the amount of genetic variation in a population associated with variation in the expression of some trait) is not instinct (an inherited stereotyped behavior pattern like the nest-building activities of a bird); 5) traits as distributions of scores; and 6) distributions as moments or the mathematical descriptions of their major features, such as average, scatter, asymmetry and peakedness.

Since genetic inheritance comes to us in bits and pieces, as it were, not in a lump, the hereditary endowment of each individual is a unique mosaic—an assemblage of factors many of which are independent. Because of the lotterylike nature of fertilization and even of the way egg and sperm are formed, no two individuals other than identical twins share the same genotypic mosaic.

The ontogeny of an individual's phenotype (the

observable outcome of development) has a norm or range of reaction not predictable in advance. In most cases the norm of reaction remains largely unknown, but the concept is nevertheless of fundamental importance, because it saves us from being taken in by glib and misleading textbook cliches such as "heredity sets the limits, but environment determines the extent of development within those limits." Even when, as in plants and some animals, an individual genotype can be replicated many times and its development studied over a range of environmental conditions, we can only get an approximate estimate of what the range of the genotype's reaction might be. The more varied the conditions, the more varied might be the end product. Of course, different genotypes should not be expected to have the same norm of reaction (the same seed develops into quite a different plant at sea level and above the timberline). Unfortunately, psychology's attention was diverted from appreciating this basic fact of biology by a half century of misguided environmentalism. Just as we see that, except for twins born of the same egg, no two human faces are alike, so we must expect norms of reaction to show genotypic uniqueness. That is one reason why the heroic but ill-fated attempts of experimental learning psychologists to write the "laws of environmental influence" were grasping at shadows. Those "limits set by heredity" in the textbook cliche can never be specified. They are plastic within each individual and differ between individuals. Extreme environmentalists were wrong to hope that one law or set of laws would be found that could describe universally how genetic endowment is modified. Extreme hereditarians were wrong to ignore the norm of reaction.

Individuals occur in populations, and then only as temporary attachments, so to speak, each to particular combinations of genes. The population, however, can endure indefinitely as a pool or reservoir of genes, maybe forever recombining to generate new individuals.

What is heritability? How is heritability estimated for intelligence or any other trait? Is heritability related to instinct? In 1872, Douglas Spalding demonstrated that the ontogeny of a bird's ability to fly is simply maturation and not the result of practice, imitation or any demonstrable kind of learning. He confined immature birds and deprived them of the opportunity either to practice flapping their wings or to observe and imitate the flight of older birds; in spite of this, they developed the ability to fly. For some ethologists this deprivation experiment became the paradigm for proving the innateness or instinctive nature of a behavior by demonstrating that it appears despite the absence of any opportunity for it to be learned. Remember two things about this approach: first, the observation involves experimental manipulation of the conditions of experience during development, and second, such observation can be made on the development of one individual. For some people the results of a deprivation experiment now constitute the operational demonstration of the existence (or nonexistence) of an instinct in a particular species.

Are instincts heritable, that is, are they determined by genes? But what is a gene? A gene is an inference from a breeding experiment. It is recognized by the measurement of individual differences—the recognition of the segregation of distinguishable forms of the expression of some trait among the progeny of appropriate matings. For example, when an individual of blood type AA mates with one of type BB, their offspring are uniformly AB. If two of the AB offspring mate, it is found that the A and B gene forms, or alleles as they are called technically, have segregated during reproduction and recombined in their progeny to produce all combinations of A and B: AA, AB and BB. Note that the only operation involved in such a study is *breeding* of one or more generations and then, at an appropriate time of life, observation of the separate individuals born in each generation—controlled breeding with experimental material or pedigree analysis of the appropriate families. In principle, only one (usually brief) observation is required. Thus we see that genetics is a science of *differences,* and the breeding experiment is its fundamental operation. The operational definition of the gene, therefore, involves observation in a breeding experiment of the segregation among several individuals of distinguishable differences in the expression of some trait from which the gene can be inferred; that is, in contrast to the study of instinct, a genetic study requires more than one subject, whose development is studied. Moreover, all discussions of genetic analysis presuppose sufficiently adequate control of environmental conditions so that all observed individual differences have developed under the same environmental conditions—conditions never achieved in any human studies.

How does heritability enter the picture? At the present stage of knowledge, many features (traits) of animals and plants have not yet been related to genes that can be recognized individually. But the role of large number of genes, often called polygenes and in most organisms still indistinguishable one from the other, has been demonstrated easily (and often) by selective breeding or by appropriate comparisons between different strains of animals or plants. Selection and strain crossing have provided the basis for many advances in agriculture, and among the new generation of research workers they are becoming standard tools for the experimental behaviorist. Heritability often summarizes the extent to which a particular population has responded to a regimen of being bred selectively on the basis of the expression of some trait, as is done for milk production in cattle and egg production in poultry. Heritability values vary on a continuum between zero and plus one. If the distribution of trait expression among progeny remains the same no matter how their parents might be selected, then heritability has zero value. If parental selection does make a difference, heritability exceeds zero, its exact value reflecting the parent-offspring correlation.

A heritability estimate, however, is a far more limited piece of information than most people realize. As was so well stated by J.L. Fuller and W.R. Thompson, "heritability is a property of populations and not of traits." In its strictest sense, a heritability measure provides for a given population an estimate of the proportion of the variance it shows in trait (phenotype) expression which is correlated with the segregation of the alleles of independently acting genes; that is, milk yield might have a high heritability in one heterogeneous herd of cattle and a very low heritability in some other relatively homogeneous herd. There are other more broadly conceived heritability measures which estimate this correlation and also include the combined effects of genes that are independent and of those that interact. Therefore, heritability estimates the proportion of individual differences shown by a trait that can be attributed to genetic variation (narrowly or broadly interpreted) in some particular population at a single generation under one set of conditions.

This description contains three fundamentally important limitations that have rarely been accorded sufficient attention. In the first place, the importance of limiting any statement about heritability to a specific population is evident when we realize that a gene, which shows variation in one population because it is represented there by two or more different forms of expression, might show no variation in some other population because it is uniformly represented there by only a single allele. Remember that initially such a gene could never have been detected by genetic methods in the second population. Once it has been detected in some population carrying two or more of its segregating alleles, the information thus obtained might permit us to recognize it in populations carrying only a single allele. Note how this is related to heritability: the trait will show a greater-than-zero heritability in the segregating population but zero heritability in the nonsegregating population. This does *not* mean that the trait is determined genetically in the first population and environmentally in the second!

Up to now my discussion has been limited to a single gene. The very same argument applies for every gene of the polygenic complexes involved in continuously varying traits like height, weight and intelligence. Also, only *genetic* variation has been considered—the presence or absence of segregating alleles at one or more loci in different populations.

Next let us consider the ever-present environmental sources of variation. Usually from the Mendelian point of view, except for the genes on the segregating chromosomes, everything inside the cell and outside the organism is lumped together and can be called environmental variation—cytoplasmic constituents, the maternal effects now known to be so important, the early experience effects studied in so many psychological laboratories and so on. None of these can be considered unimportant or trivial. They are ever present. Let us now perform what physicists call a Gedanken, or thought, experiment. Imagine Aldous Huxley's *Brave New World* or Skinner's *Walden II* organized in such a way that every individual is exposed to precisely the same environmental conditions. In other words, consider the extreme, but *un*realistic, case of complete environmental homogeneity. Under these circumstances the heritability value would approach plus one, because only genetic variation would be present. Don't forget, however, that even under these conditions, there are over 70 trillion potential human genotypes—no two of us share the same genotype no matter how many ancestors we happen to have in common. Since our unique genotype is in the nucleus, or executive, of every cell in our bodies, the individuality that is so obvious in the human faces we see around us must also characterize the unseen components. Let the same experiment be imagined for any number of environments. Since every genotype has a unique norm of reaction, they can develop differently in the different possible environments, and the rank ordering of their phenotypes will not necessarily remain the same in the different environments because the shift from one environment to another must not be expected to have the same effect on every genotype; for example, the change from hypothetical environment A to B might raise the score on some measure for one individual and lower that of another individual whereas the reverse might happen for

the same two individuals with the change from hypothetical environment A to C.

The third limitation refers to the fact that because
gene frequencies can and do change from one generation
to the next, so will heritability values or the magnitude
of the genetic variance.

Now let us shift our focus to the entire genotype or
at least to those of its components that might co-vary at
least partially with the phenotypic expression of a
particular trait. Early in this century, Woltereck, a
German zoologist, called to our attention the norm-of-
reaction concept: the same genotype can give rise to a
wide array of phenotypes depending upon the environment in which it develops. This is most conveniently
studied in plants where genotypes are easily replicated.
Later R.B. Goldschmidt, a German-American geneticist, was to show in the fruit fly that, by careful
selection of the environmental conditions at critical
periods in development, various phenotypes ordinarily
associated with specific gene mutations could be produced from genotypes that did not include the mutant
form of those genes. Descriptively, Goldschmidt called
these events *phenocopies*—environmentally produced
imitations of gene mutants or phenotypic expressions
only manifested by the "inappropriate" genotype if
unusual environmental influences impinge during critical
periods in development, but regularly manifested by the
"appropriate" genotype under the usual environmental
conditions.

In 1946, the brilliant British geneticist J.B.S. Haldane
analyzed the interaction concept and gave quantitative
meaning to the foregoing. For the simplest case but one,
that of two genotypes in three environments, or for its
mathematical equivalent, that of three genotypes in two

environments, he showed that there are 60 possible
kinds of interaction. Ten genotypes in ten environments
generate 10^{144} possible kinds of interaction. In general,
m genotypes in n environments generate $(mn)!/m!n!$
kinds of interaction. Since the characterization of
genotype-environment interaction can only be ad hoc (is
unpredictable and therefore only can be described after
it has happened) and the number of possible interactions is effectively unlimited, it is no wonder that the
long search for general laws has been so unfruitful.

For genetically different lines of rats that had been
bred to be "bright" or "dull" in the preformance of a
given task, by so simple a change in environmental
conditions as increasing the interval of the time allowed
between practice trials, J.U. McGaugh, R.D. Jennings
and C.W. Thompson found that the so-called dulls
moved right up to the scoring level of the so-called
brights. In a recent study of the open-field behavior of
mice, J.P. Hegmann and J.C. DeFries found that
heritabilities measured repeatedly in the same individuals were unstable over two successive days. In survey-
ing earlier work, they commented: "Heritability estimates for repeated measurements of behavioral characters have been found to increase (Broadhurst and Jinks,
1961), decrease (Broadhurst and Jinks, 1966), and
fluctuate randomly (Fuller and Thompson, 1960) as a
function of repeated testing." Therefore, to the limitations on heritability due to population, situation and
breeding generation, we must now add developmental
stage, or, many people might say, just plain unreliabil-
ity! The late and brilliant Sir Ronald Fisher, whose
authority Jensen cites, indicated how fully he had
appreciated such limitations when he commented: "the
so-called co-efficient of heritability, which I regard as

one of those unfortunate short-cuts which have emerged in biometry for lack of a more thorough analysis of the data." The plain facts are that in the study of man a heritability estimate turns out to be a piece of "knowledge" that is both deceptive and trivial.

The other two concepts to be taken into account when racial comparisons are considered involve for each population (race) the description by a distribution of the scores obtained by individuals when some trait (like intelligence) has been measured and the use of statistical measures (like moments) to describe those distributions. Populations should be compared only with respect to one trait at a time, and comparisons should be made in terms of the moment statistics of their trait distributions. Therefore, for any two populations, on each trait of interest, a separate comparison should be made for every moment of their score distributions. If we consider only the first four moments, from which are derived the familiar statistics for mean, variance, skewness and kurtosis, then there are four ways in which populations or races may differ with respect to any single trait. Since we possess 23 independently assorting pairs of chromosomes, certainly there are at least 23 uncorrelated traits with respect to which populations can be compared. Since comparisons will be made in terms of four (usually independent) statistics, there are $4 \times 23 = 92$ ways in which races can differ. Since the integrity of chromosomes is *not* preserved over the generations, because they often break apart at meiosis and exchange constituent genes, there are far more than 23 independent hereditary units. If instead of 23 chromosomes we take the 100,000 genes man is now estimated to possess, and we think in terms of their phenotypic trait correlates, then there may be as many as 400,000 comparisons to be made between any two populations or races.

A priori, at this time we know enough to expect no two populations to be the same with respect to most or all of the constituents of their gene pools. Mutations and recombinations will occur at different places, at different times and with differing frequencies. Furthermore, selection pressures will also vary. So the number and kinds of differences between populations now waiting to be revealed in "the more thorough analysis" recommended by R. A. Fisher literally stagger the imagination. It does not suggest a linear hierarchy of inferior and superior races.

Why has so much stress been placed on comparing distributions only with respect to their average values? There is so much evidence that many distributions of observations differ with respect to other features besides their averages. The source of our difficulty traces back to the very inception of our statistical tradition.

There is an unbroken line of intellectual influence from Quetelet through Galton and Pearson to modern psychometrics and biometrics. Adolphe Quetelet (1796-1874), the Belgian astronomer-statistician, introduced the concept of "the average man"; he also applied the normal distribution, so widely used in astronomy for error variation, to human data, biological and social. The great Francis Galton followed Quetelet's lead, and then Karl Pearson elaborated and perfected their methods. I know of nothing that has contributed more to impose and perpetuate the typological way of thought on present-day psychology than the feedback from these methods for describing observations in terms of group averages.

There is a technique called composite photography to
the perfection of which Sir Francis Galton contributed
in an important way. Some of Galton's best work in this
field was done by combining—literally averaging—the
separate physiognomic features of many different Jewish individuals into his composite photograph of "the
Jewish type." Karl Pearson, his disciple and biographer,
wrote: "There is little doubt that Galton's Jewish type
formed a landmark in composite photography." The
part played by typological thinking in the development
of modern statistics and the way in which such
typological thinking has been feeding back into our
conceptual framework through our continued careless
use of these statistics are illuminated by Galton's
following remarks:

> The word generic presupposes a genus, that is to say,
> a collection of individuals who have much in com-
> mon, and among whom medium characteristics are
> very much more frequent than extreme ones. The
> same idea is sometimes expressed by the word
> typical, which was much used by Quetelet, who was
> the first to give it a rigorous interpretation, and
> whose idea of a type lies at the basis of his statistical
> views. No statistician dreams of combining objects
> into the same generic group that do not cluster
> towards a common centre; no more can we compose
> generic portraits out of heterogeneous elements, for
> if the attempt be made to do so the result is
> monstrous and meaningless.

The basic assumption of a type, or typical individual, is
clear and explicit. They used the normal curve, and they
permitted distributions to be represented by an average
because, even though at times they knew better, far too

often they tended to think of races as discrete, even homogeneous, groups and individual variation as error.

It is important to realize that these developments began before 1900, when Mendel's work was still unknown. Thus at the inception of biosocial science there was no substantive basis for understanding individual differences. After 1900, when Mendel's work became available, its incorporation into biosocial science was bitterly opposed by the biometricians under Pearson's leadership. Galton had promulgated two "laws": his law of ancestral heredity (1865) and his law of regression (1877). When G.U. Yule, a British statistician, and W.E. Castle, an American geneticist, pointed out how the law of ancestral heredity could be explained in Mendelian terms, Pearson stubbornly denied it. Mendel had chosen for experimental observation seven traits, each of which, in his pea plant material, turned out to be a phenotypic correlate of a single gene with two segregating alleles. For all seven traits one allele was dominant. Unfortunately, Pearson assumed the universality of dominance and based his disdain for Mendelism on this assumption. Yule then showed that without the assumption of dominance, Mendelism becomes perfectly consistent with the kind of quantitative data on the basis of which it was being rejected by Pearson. It is sad to realize that Pearson never appreciated the generality of Mendelism and seems to have gone on for the next 32 years without doing so.

Now we can consider the recent debate about the meaning of comparisons between the "intelligence" of different human races. We are told that intelligence has a high heritability and that one race performs better than another on intelligence tests. In essence we are presented with a racial hierarchy reminiscent of that pernicious "system" which John Langdon Haydon Down used when he misnamed a disease entity "mongolism."

The people who are so committed to answering the nature-nurture pseudoquestion "Is heredity or environment more important in determining intelligence?" make two conceptual blunders. Like Spalding's question about the instinctive nature of bird flight, which introduced the ethologists's deprivation experiment, their question about intelligence is, in fact, being asked about the development of a single individual. Unlike Spalding and the ethologists, however, they do not study development in single individuals. Usually they test groups of individuals at a single time of life. The weights being assigned to heredity and to environment refer to the relative amounts of the variance between individuals comprising a population, not how much of whatever enters into the development of the observed expression of a trait in a particular individual has been contributed by heredity and by environment, respectively. They want to know how instinctive is intelligence in the development of a certain individual, but instead they measure differences between large numbers of fully, or partially, developed individuals. If we now take into consideration the norm-of-reaction concept and combine it with the facts of genotypic individuality, then there is no general statement that can be made about the assignment of fixed proportions to the contributions of heredity and environment either to the development of a single individual, because we have not even begun to assess his norm of reaction, or to the differences that might be measured among members of a population, because we have hardly begun to assess the range of environmental conditions under which its constituent members might develop!

Their second mistake—an egregious error—is related to the first one. They assume an inverse relationship between heritability magnitude and improvability by training and teaching. If heritability is high, little room is left for improvement by environmental modification. If heritability is low, much more improvement is possible. Note how this basic fallacy is incorporated directly into the title of Jensen's article "How Much Can We Boost IQ and Scholastic Achievement?" To that question he gave a straightforward, but fallacious, answer: "The fact that scholastic achievement is considerably less heritable than intelligence . . . means there is potentially much more we can do to improve school performance through environmental means than we can do to change intelligence." Commenting on the heritability of intelligence and "the old nature-nurture controversy," one of Jensen's respondents makes the same mistake in his rebuttal: "This is an old estimate which many of us have used, but we have used it to determine what could be done with the variance left for the some of the implications of environmental variance for education and child rearing."

The trouble with this is that high or low heritability tells us absolutely nothing about how a given individual might have developed under conditions different from those in which he actually did develop. Heritability provides no information about norm of reaction. Since the characterization of genotype-environment interaction can only be ad hoc and the number of possible interactions is effectively unlimited, no wonder the search for general laws of behavior has been so unfruitful—and *the* heritability of intelligence or of any other trait must be recognized as still another of those will-o'-the-wisp general laws. And no magic words about an interaction component in a linear analysis-of-variance model will make disappear the reality of each geno-type's unique norm of reaction. Such claims by Jensen or anyone else are false. Interaction is an abstraction of mathematics. Norm of reaction is a developmental reality of biology in plants, animals and people.

In Israel, the descendants of those Jews Pearson feared would contaminate Britain are manifesting some interesting properties of the norm of reaction. According to B.S. Bloom, children of European origin have an average IQ of 105 when they are brought up in individual homes. Those brought up in a kibbutz on the nursery rearing schedule of 22 hours per day for four or more years have an average IQ of 115. In contrast, the Middle-Eastern Jewish children brought up in individual homes have an average IQ of only 85, Jensen's danger point. However, when brought up in a kibbutz they also have an average IQ of 115; that is, they perform the same as the European children with whom they were matched for education, the occupational level of parents and the kibbutz group in which they were raised. There is no basis for expecting different overall results for any population in our species.

The Role of Experience in the Development of Competence

J. McVICKER HUNT

What determines human intelligence? What determines the competence of people? Is it fixed and immutable at a child's birth? Or does it change with time and circumstance? If it does, then what circumstances will best foster its maximum growth?

These questions once agitated only a small group of scholars and scientists. No longer. Today they have acquired urgent social and political significance. The fates of vast programs and many a career may hinge on the conclusions of the most recondite social-psychological study. A scholarly paper, a thicket of statistical tables, becomes an object of burning interest for journalists, politicians and others concerned to find "the" answer to why the children of the poor don't seem to learn as much in school as their own children do.

I had thought, though, that at least in the years since

World War II we had learned something about most of these matters. I had thought we had learned that it was no longer tenable to conceive of intelligence tests as indicators of fixed capacity or innate potential in children. I had thought we had learned that it was quite wrong to think we could predict an adult's intellectual competence from his score on a test taken as a child without specifying the circumstances he would encounter in the interim.

In fact our political and educational leaders do seem to have gotten this message. The circumstances that affect a child's experiences in the course of growing up *are* believed to play an important role in affecting intelligence and the motivation for achievement and competence. This notion has been used in formulating solutions to the crisis of the cities created by the heavy migration of the poor from the South. Only a little imagination and goodwill has been needed to infer that the children of lower socioeconomic backgrounds, once very widely considered to be innately stupid and lazy, may instead be viewed as children who have been cheated of that equality of opportunity which our forefathers considered to be the birthright of all.

Unfortunately, however, these changing conceptions of intelligence and growth appear to have reached the leaders even before they have been fully appreciated among those of us trained in the psychological sciences. I say "unfortunately" because the newer conceptions may have led to excessive hopes among politicians and the administrators of our educational systems. Too many of them have a tendency to confuse the perfectly justifiable expectation that there can be significant improvement in the competence of the children of the poor with the basic scientific know-how required to carry out, or even to plan, the broad educational programs needed to do the job. What I am worried about is that the confusion and excessive hopes may have created an "oversell" that will now be followed by an "overkill" of support for the efforts to develop and deploy effective educational programs. One has only to recall the recent vicissitudes of the Head Start program.

Moreover, the possibility of an overkill is made all the more dangerous by the revival of interest and belief in the notion that races differ in inherited potential for competence. People so persuaded are far from extinct. We all witnessed the great flurry of attention given by the national press to Arthur Jensen's recent paper on the relative immutability of the IQ. Although one cannot with certainty rule out the possibility of racial differences in potential for competence, the whole issue is of very little import so long as the great majority of black, Puerto Rican and Indian children grow up in poverty with extremely limited opportunities to acquire the language and number abilities and the motivation that underlie full participation in our society.

But I am no less fearful that the failure of some of our most expensive and publicized efforts to improve dramatically the learning potential of poor children may lead to an unjustified discouragement on the part not only of politicians but of the public that must pay for these efforts. I am afraid that our ignorance of how to proceed effectively may now deprive us, for an indefinite period, of the opportunity to do what I am confident ultimately can be done to meet these challenges. What we need is the opportunity to innovate and evaluate, to fail, to correct our misinterpretations and our failures, and gradually to develop programs of educational technology, beginning even at birth, that *are* effective in fostering development.

It is these concerns that have prompted me to review here the evidence for the crucial importance of life's circumstances for the development of the cognitive skills and the attitudes that comprise competence.

It should have been obvious from the beginning that scores on tests of intelligence could not possibly serve as indicators of hereditary capacity or potential. It is a truism to say that one's genetic endowment sets limits on intellectual potential and also that it greatly influences what happens when we encounter any given series of circumstances. As a scientific statement, however, this is basically meaningless, as Alfred Binet, the developer of the most widely used IQ test, recognized as early as 1909 when he struck out against

... some recent philosophers [who] appear to have given their moral support to this deplorable verdict that the intelligence of an individual is a fixed quantity ... we must protest and act against this brutal pessimism ... (for) a child's mind is like a field for which an expert farmer has advised a change in the methods of cultivation, with the result that in the place of a desert land, we now have a harvest. It is in this particular sense, the one which is significant, that we say that the intelligence of children may be increased. One increases that which constitutes the intelligence of a school child, namely the capacity to learn, to improve with instruction.

Although the complex tests of Binet and Theodore Simon remained pre-eminent in the intelligence-testing movement, the conceptual framework built up around their use was developed by the students of Francis

Galton and G. Stanley Hall, rather than by Binet. This framework emphasized from the beginning the role of heredity as a fixer of intelligence and a predeterminant of development in the interpretation of test scores.

Moreover, throughout more than the first four decades of this century, American textbooks on genetics tended to emphasize the work of Gregor Mendel on the hereditary transmission of traits and to neglect the work of Walter Johannsen on the crucial role of the inter-action of the *genotype* (the constellation of genes received by an organism from its progenitors) with the environment in determining the *phenotype* (the observable characteristics of an organism).

To be sure, some of the early evidence did seem to confirm the notion of intelligence tests as indicators of adult capacity. For instance, the IQs of groups of children showed great constancy (which was a consequence of the way the tests were constructed) and also considerable individual constancy once a child got into school. Moreover, efforts at training children directly on the intellectual functions tested turned out to have but short-lived effects. Furthermore, the IQs of persons closely related to a child proved to be more similar than the IQs of persons less closely related or unrelated.

Since World War II, however, evidence has been accumulated that is so out of keeping with the belief that the tests indicated fixed innate capacity or potential that the belief is no longer tenable.

Perhaps the most incontrovertible of this evidence is that of rising intelligence in the face of predicted deterioration. The prediction of deterioration came from combining two observations. First, it has been obvious since the seventeenth century that poor families have more children than families of the middle and upper classes. Second, many studies have shown that people from low socioeconomic background typically average about 20 points of IQ below people in the upper-middle class. In 1937, R. B. Cattell multiplied the number of people at each IQ level by the reproduction rate at that level and computed the new mean to estimate the IQ of the next generation. From this procedure, he estimated a drop of a little over three points a generation, or about one point a decade. This he characterized as a "galloping plunge toward intellectual bankruptcy."

But Cattell's dire prediction has been repeatedly contradicted by rising IQs in those populations where the children of a given age have been tested and retested after intervals of a decade or more. Thirteen years after his own forecast, Cattell himself published a study comparing ten-year-old children living in the city of Leicester, England in 1949 with the ten-year-old children living in that same city in 1936. In the place of the predicted drop of something slightly more than one point in IQ, Cattell acutally found an increase of 1.28 points. Although small, this increase was highly significant from the statistical standpoint.

In other studies, the predicted drop in IQ has been proven wrong by gains substantially larger than these. S. Smith reported a growth of around 20 points between the scores of children in various Honolulu schools in 1924 and the scores of children in those same schools in 1938. Lester Wheeler reported a ten-point increase in the mean IQ of children from a single group of families in the ten-year period before and after the great changes brought about in that community by the Tennessee Valley Authority. When Frank Finch compared the IQs of all students in a sample of high schools in the 1920s and again in those same high schools in the 1940s, he found the average gains ranging between 10 and 15 points. But perhaps the most dramatic evidence of an upward shift came when the test performances of soldiers in World War II were compared with those of World War I soldiers. Clearly, if the tests measure fixed intellectual capacity or innate potential, and if the majority of each new generation comes from parents in the lowest third in tested intelligence, something very, very strange is happening.

It has long been customary to differentiate intelligence tests from achievement tests. Some differences do exist. All are differences in degree, however, rather than in kind.

First, intelligence tests tend to tap a wider variety of experience, both in and out of school, than do achievement tests. Most achievement tests are closely tied to specific courses of study. Intelligence tests are not. School experience still contributes, however, to performance on more broadly based tests of intelligence. Moreover, experiences in the home and in social groups contribute to performance on achievement tests. Second, achievement tests are aimed at relatively new learning, while intelligence tests depend typically on older learning.

Intelligence tests and achievement tests, then, are measures of current capacity depending directly upon previously acquired skills and information and motivation. Binet saw this at the turn of the century, but he had escaped the "advantages" of the tutelage of men with strong theoretical beliefs in intelligence fixed by heredity.

Semantics can often have unfortunate consequences. The terms "dimensions" and "scale" when applied to such matters as intelligence are a case in point. These terms were borrowed from measurement in the physical world where scales are instruments for measuring unvarying dimensions. When these terms are applied to the behavior of people, we tend also to apply notions of concreteness and constancy derived from the world of physical objects. Thus, calling intelligence a dimension of behavior and speaking of tests as scales tends to obscure reality. This becomes especially unfortunate when the semantics sap the motivation of teachers to change their approaches to promote increased development in children who resist their standard approaches and curricula.

Let me turn next to those propositions concerning development that I believe are no longer tenable and that I believe are highly unfortunate in their influence upon those working in programs of early childhood education.

Fallacy: the rate of development is predetermined. I am confident that belief in a predetermined rate of human development is quite untenable. In the history of our thinking about psychological development, the constant IQ was the epitome of this notion. But it got support from the widely cited work of G. E. Coghill in the 1920s which related developmental sequences in the behavior of salamander larvae from head to tail and from trunk to limbs to microscopic histological evidences of neuromuscular maturation. Support also came from various other observations that I cannot take time to review here. Suffice it to say that maturation and learning were seen as two distinctly separate processes with maturation predetermined by heredity and learning controlled by the circumstances encountered.

Evidence contradicting the notion of a predetermined rate of development also appeared. Wendell Cruze reported that chicks allowed to peck for only 15 minutes a day failed to improve in the accuracy of their pecking. Moreover, the early longitudinal studies of intellectual development in children uncovered individual growth curves with changes in IQ as large as 60 points. Several students in the 1930s found increases in the IQs of young children associated with nursery schooling.

At the time, however, the credibility of these observations of change in the rate of development was questioned by other observers who posited differing inherited patterns of growth or found methodological weaknesses in the studies. Differences of more than 20 points of IQ were found between identical twins reared apart under differing kinds of circumstances, but, because such instances were rare, they were considered to be merely examples of errors of measurement.

One of the most impressive of the early studies to cast doubt on the notion of a predetermined rate of development is that of Harold M. Skeels and Murlon H. Dye. This study was prompted by a "clinical surprise." Two residents of a state orphanage, one aged 13 months With a Kühlmann IQ of 46 and the other aged 16 months with an IQ of 35, were committed to an institution for the retarded. After six months there, where the mentally retarded women doted on them, these two children showed a remarkably rapid rate of development. Coupled with change from apathy to liveliness was an improvement of 31 points of IQ in one and 52 points in the other. After this, a group of 13 infants—ranging in age from 7 months to 30 months and in IQs from 36 to 89, with a mean of 64—were transferred from the orphanage (but not committed) to these wards for moron women. After being there for periods ranging from 6 months for the seven-month-old child to 52 months for the 30-month-old child, every one of these infants showed a gain in IQ. The minimum gain was 7 points; the maximum was 58 points, and all but four showed gains of over 20 points.

On the other hand, 12 other infants—ranging in age from 12 to 22 months and in IQ from 50 to 103, with a mean IQ of 87—were left in the orphanage. When these infants were retested after periods varying from 20 to 43 months, all but one of them showed decreases in IQ that ranged from eight to 45 points, and five of the decreases exceeded 35 points. These findings suggested strongly that the effects of these two institutional environments differed greatly, but the idea that children's IQs had been improved by moving them from an orphanage to a school for the mentally retarded was merely ridiculed, and the ridicule deprived the findings of their highly suggestive import.

In the light of the evidence accumulated since World War II, this study of Skeels and Dye has acquired the status of a classic, and the notion of a predetermined rate of development has become almost incredible.

Fallacy: maturation is independent of circumstances. Locomotor development has long been considered to be predetermined, but in 1957 Wayne Dennis discovered an orphanage in Tehran where 60 percent of those infants in their second year were still not sitting up alone and where 84 percent of those in their fourth year were still not walking. When one considers that nearly all family-reared infants are sitting alone at eight months and nearly all such infants are walking alone by 20 months of age, it becomes clear that locomotor development cannot be independent of circumstances.

In the 1940s, the theorizing of Donald Hebb prompted investigators to rear animals under circumstances varying in complexity, especially in perceptual complexity. In the first such study, Hebb himself found the adult ability of rats reared as pets to be superior in solving maze problems to that of litter-mates reared in laboratory cages. Other investigators have found that dogs reared freely in complex environments are better as adults at learning mazes than their litter-mates reared in the monotony of laboratory cages.

The neuropsychological theorizing of Hebb and the theorizing of Holger Hydén, a Swedish biochemist, have prompted investigators to rear animals in the dark and in environments of various levels of complexity to determine the effects of such variations in rearing on both behavioral development and neuroanatomical maturation. Dark-reared chimpanzees, cats, rabbits, rats and mice have all shown deficiencies of both nerve cells and glial cells of their retinal ganglia when compared with animals or litter-mates reared in the light of laboratory cages. More recent investigations have extended these neuroanatomical deficiencies associated with dark-rearing to the appropriate nuclei of the thalamus and even to the striate area of the occipital lobe of the brain. These highly exciting finds indicate that even neuroanatomical maturation can no longer be considered to be independent of the circumstances in which animals develop.

Fallacy: longitudinal prediction is possible. Despite such an accumulation of evidence as I have indicated (and there is much more), the belief in a constant IQ has given us the habit of thinking of the validity of tests in longitudinal terms. We have used and still use the scores based on the performance of children on tests administered at one age to predict what their school or test performances will be at later ages.

Yet, if even neuroanatomic maturation can be influenced by circumstances, and if psychological development is as plastic as this evidence implies, longitudinal prediction is impossible from test scores alone. The plasticity that appears to exist in the rate at which human organisms develop renders longitudinal prediction basically impossible unless one specifies the circumstances under which this development is to take place. In fact, trying to predict what a person's IQ will be at 20 on the basis of his IQ at age one or two is like trying to predict how heavy a two-week-old calf will be when he is a two-year-old without knowing whether he will be reared in a dry pasture, in an irrigated pasture or in a feed lot.

To be sure, longitudinal prediction improves with age. This results from the fact that test-retest validities involve part-whole relationships. Thus, if one is predicting IQ at 20, the older the child is at the time of the initial test, the larger becomes the predictor part of the criterion whole. Moreover, in actual situations, individuals tend to remain within sets of social, economic and educational circumstances that are relatively stable. Thus, a very large share of whatever constancy individual IQs have had can be attributed to a combination of the increasingly congruent part-whole relationship and with the sameness of circumstances.

Belief in a predetermined rate of development and in the possibility of predicting performance over time has had very unfortunate consequences for educational practice. When children fail to learn and are found to have low scores on intelligence tests, teachers are prompt to feel that "these children are doing as well as can be expected." Such an attitude dampens any inclination teachers may have to alter their approach to such children. Consequence? The tutelage that the child encounters remains essentially stable, and the child continues in his rut of failure.

An important corollary of the finding that the rate of development depends upon the circumstances encountered is a needed change in the conception of "readiness." The notion that children are ready for certain kinds of experiences and not for others had validity. On the other hand, the notion that this "readiness" is a matter of predetermined maturation, as distinct from learning or past encounters with circumstances, is basically wrong and potentially damaging. What is involved is what I have been calling "the problem of the match." If encountering a given set of circumstances is to induce psychological development in the child, these circumstances must have an appropriate relationship to the information and skills already accumulated by the child. This is no easy matter. Ordinarily, the best indicators of an appropriate match are to be found, I now believe, in emotional behavior. They are evidences of interest and of mild surprise. If the circumstances are too simple and too familiar, the child will fail to develop and he is likely to withdraw into boredom. If the circumstances demand too much of a child, he will withdraw in fear or explode in anger. So long as the child can withdraw from the circumstances without facing punishment, loss of love, fear of disapproval, or what-not, I believe it is impossible to overstimulate him.

The challenge in such a conception of "readiness" as that involved in the "problem of the match" is basically the problem of preparing the environment to foster development. We are a long way from solid knowledge of how to do this, but I believe we do have some sensible suggestions about how to proceed.

One more point about development and its implications. Order has always been obvious in behavioral development. In locomotor development, for instance, it is obvious that the infant is at first rooted to a given spot, that he learns to wheel and twist before he sits up, that he sits up alone before he can creep, that he creeps or scoots before he stands, that he stands before he cruises, that he cruises while holding on to things before he toddles, that he toddles before he walks, and that he walks before he runs. Arnold Gesell and his collaborators at Yale devoted their total normative enterprise to describing the order in the various domains of behavioral development that take place with advancing age. Jean Piaget and his collaborators have also been concerned with describing the order in intelligence and in the construction of such aspects of reality as object permanence, as constancy of quantity, of shape, and of color, and causality, space and time. Ina Uzgiris and I have been using these orderly landmarks in development as a basis for our ordinal scales of psychological development in infancy. In short, order in development is an obvious fact.

Although Gesell gave occasional lip service to the interaction between child and environment in behavioral development, all but one of his various principles of growth (that of "individuating maturation") described predetermined processes. Moreover, in 1954 Gesell explicitly said that "the so-called environment, whether internal or external, does not generate the progressions of development. Environmental factors support, inflect and specify; but they do not engender the basic forms and sequences of ontogenesis."

Similarly, Mary Shirley saw evidence of Coghill's head-to-tail principle when she wrote that "motor control begins headward and travels toward the feet beginning with the eye muscle and progressing through stages in which the head and neck muscles are mastered, arms and upper trunk come under control . . . the baby at last achieves mastery of his whole body. . . ."

Yet such an interpretation is not a necessary implication of the observed fact of orderliness in development. While Piaget, like Gesell, has found order in psychological development, he, unlike Gesell, has emphasized the role of interaction. According to Piaget, development occurs in the course of adaptive interaction between the child and the environment. This interaction involves two complimentary and invariant processes: *assimilation* and *accommodation*. Piaget conceives these processes as basically common to the physiological as well as the psychological domain. Assimilation occurs whenever an organism utilizes something from the environment and incorporates it into its own structures. Accommodation, the complement of assimilation, operates whenever encounters with the environment evoke a change in the existing structure of the central processes that mediate the interpretation of events and control action. Thus, accommodation is another term for adaptive learning.

Although I cannot here go into Piaget's ideas, they have definitely influenced my own thinking about learning. Attempting to understand them has opened my own eyes to the fact that circumstances influence development in ways quite other than those within the traditional rubrics under which we have studied learning.

Learning in poverty. As I have already noted, the factors controlling the development of competence in early childhood are no longer purely an academic topic. These factors have acquired both social and political significance from the fact that our advancing technology is rapidly decreasing the economic opportunities for those without linguistic and mathematical abilities, the motivation to solve problems and the inclination to carry social responsibility, and from the fact that a large number of black people, coming from a background of poverty and limited opportunity, lack these skills and motives. In the light of these challenges, what are the implications of the foregoing argument?

The intellectual capacity that underlies competence in substantial part is not fixed. In this connection, various lines of evidence suggest strongly that being reared in conditions of poverty and cultural deprivation deprives a child of opportunities to learn. The children of poor families have typically encountered many fewer kinds of objects than children of the middle class. As infants, the children of poverty often have inadequate diets and they live in crowded circumstances which expose them to a continuous vocal racket to which they become habituated. This habituation may account for the inadequacies in hearing other people speak that was found by Cynthia Deutsch and by Deutsch and Brown. Too often, the verbal interaction of children of the poor with their elders is limited to commands to stop whatever the child is doing without explanations as to why. Seldom are these children invited to note what is going on around them or to formulate their observations in their own language. These children are especially unlikely to learn the syntactical rules of the standard language. Seldom is their ingenuity rewarded except when they learn to avoid the punishment that comes when they get caught at something arbitrarily prohibited. In such circumstances, the low test scores repeatedly observed in the children of poverty are to be expected.

With respect to motivation, moreover, the children of poverty, black or white, have little opportunity to learn to take initiative, to give up present satisfactions for larger satisfactions in the future, or to take pride in problem-solving achievement. Seldom have the poor acquired such motives. Thus, their responses to their children's demands are dictated largely by their own immediate impulses and needs, not the children's. To these parents, a good child is typically a quiet child who does not bother them.

Regarding conduct, finally, these children of the poor are exposed to circumstances and standards that are hardly those prescribed by the demands of the dominant society. The models of behavior for these children often make them unfit for adaptation to either schools or marketplace. So long as a large percentage of black people are reared in poverty under these conditions of childrearing it is not tenable to attribute to race the existing deficiency in competence as measured by intelligence tests.

From such evidence as has been accumulating on the matter of class differences in child-rearing, it is becoming clearer and clearer that the accident of being born in poverty serves to deprive children of that equality of opportunity which our founding fathers considered to be the right of all Americans.

What is to be done? These relatively new findings concerning the role of circumstances in the development of competence suggest that corrective efforts should be focused upon the young, and preferably upon the very young—even beginning with birth. These findings suggest that early childhood education can have tremendous social significance if we learn how to do it effectively. It is a long step, however, from justifiable hopes to the development of the educational technology in workable form and to its broad-scale deployment in America. The question is, can we extend these findings into programs of early childhood education fast enough?

Project Head Start was a fine step in the right direction. The danger is that it may have been taken with hopes too high before an adequately effective technology of early childhood education for the children of the poor had been developed. All too often, the Head Start programs have merely supplied poor children with an opportunity to play in traditional nursery schools that were designed chiefly to exercise large muscles and to enable middle-class children to escape from their overly strict and solicitous mothers. Such opportunities are unlikely to be very effective in overcoming the deficient skills and motives to be found in the children of the poor.

Nursery schools were invented originally for the purposes of compensatory education. Shortly after the turn of the century, Maria Montessori developed a program for the poor children of the San Lorenzo district of Rome which appeared to be highly successful. She provided a practical solution to what I am calling the "problem of the match" by breaking the lock-step in education and permitting each child to follow his own interests in working with a variety of materials that she had found to be stimulating to children. She arranged these materials in sequences that would lead to conceptual skills. Moreover, in her classes she combined children ranging in age from three to six and thereby provided the younger with a graded series of models for imitation and the older ones with opportunities to learn by helping to teach the younger. Somewhat later, Margaret McMillan established her nursery schools in the slums of England to give these children, whom she considered to be environmentally handicapped, an opportunity to learn many of the abilities and motives that children of the middle class learn spontaneously. When the nursery schools were brought to the United States, however, it was only the well-to-do who could pay for them. Our traditional belief that class differences in ability are the inevitable consequence of heredity left Americans with little inclination to provide nursery schools for children of the poor. Thus, the schools got adapted to what were conceived to be the needs of the middle-class children. When the decision to mount Project Head Start was made, only these programs were widely available for deployment on a large scale. It should be no surprise, then, if the success of Project Head Start in improving the future academic success of children of the poor is highly limited.

In consequence of this unfortunate history, we have no ready-made technology of compensatory early childhood education designed to foster in children of the poor those abilities and motives underlying competence in the dominant society which circumstances prevented their acquiring.

This is beginning to be recognized. With the recognition is coming a tremendous explosion in new curricula for young children. My impression is that these achieve little unless they focus on the fostering of the ability to handle language and number concepts, and, with regard to motivation, on extending the time interval in which these children operate psychologically, and on developing pride in achievement. I see no substitute for a painstaking investigation of what works and what does not work coupled with a theoretical synthesis calculated to give us a more accurate picture of the various kinds of deficits to be found in children of the slums and more effective ways either to compensate for these deficits or to prevent them.

I am inclined to believe that we shall have to extend our programs to include children of ages less than four. I believe we shall have to involve the help of parents in these programs. Attempts to influence the child-rearing of parents of the lowest socioeconomic status by means of psychotherapy-like counseling have regularly failed. On the other hand, involving parents first as observers and then as aides in nursery schools, where they get an opportunity to see the effects of new (to them) ways of dealing with children and where these techniques are explained and tried out first in school and then in home demonstrations, all this appears to be highly promising. Here the investigations of Rupert Klaus and Susan Gray and their colleagues at the George Peabody College for teachers in Nashville, Tennessee, of Ira Gordon at the University of Florida, of Merle Karnes at the University of Illinois, and of David Weikart at Ypsilanti, Michigan appear to be showing the way. In a summer nursery school for children of poverty in Nashville, for instance, Klaus and Gray have developed a curriculum that aimed at teaching language and number skills and the attitudes and motives required to cope with elementary schools. Home visitors brought each mother to observe and later to participate in the teaching at the nursery school. The home visitors interpreted for the mothers what they saw the teachers doing. Then, during the period between summer sessions of the nursery school, the home visitors saw each of the mothers every other week. During these visits, they demonstrated for the mothers such matters as how to read a story with enthusiasm, how to reinforce children for new abilities, and how to talk with children about such homemaking operations as peeling potatoes while in the process.

This effort has been evaluated by means of gains in scores on standard tests of intelligence and will be evaluated in terms of the later progress of these children in the schools. Tests given before and after the summer nursery school have shown spurts in scores of the nursery schoolers that do not appear in the test performances of the children who did not go to the nursery school.

The test results of this program also show two other highly promising phenomena. First, the younger siblings of the children going to nursery school whose mothers saw the home visitors regularly have turned out to be significantly superior in test performance to the younger siblings of the four-year-old children in two contrast groups who got neither nursery school nor the home visits. This finding suggests that the mother must have been learning something about child-rearing that generalized to their management of their younger children.

Second, the younger children of the mothers in the

contrast group who lived in the same neighborhood as those receiving the home visits got higher test scores than did the children of mothers in a contrast group living some 60 miles away. This finding suggests that mothers who learn new child-rearing practices from their observations at the nursery school and from the home visitor were somehow communicating them to their neighbors with whom they had face-to-face relationships.

The evidence is highly promising from these new efforts in compensatory education. But after Head Start we should beware of the flush of too-high hopes. I fear that the very limited success to be expected from the deployment of nursery schools designed chiefly for the children of the middle class may lead to an unjustified discouragement on the part of both political leaders and the public. I fear a fading out of support for efforts in the domain of early childhood education. At this stage of history, it is extremely important that both political leaders and voters understand the limited nature of our knowledge about how to foster competence in the young, that they understand the basis for our justified hopes, and that they comprehend the need for the continued support of fundamental research and of the process of developing an adequate technology of early childhood education. Only with continued support for research and development in this domain can we expect to create effective means of compensating for and/or preventing the deficiencies of early experience required to meet the twin challenges of racial discrimination and poverty.

June 1969

FURTHER READING:

The Disadvantaged Child: Studies of the Social Environment and the Learning Process by Martin Deutsch (New York: Basic Books, 1967) is an anthology of many of the pioneering developments in early childhood education.

Studies in Cognitive Development: Essays in the Honor of Jean Piaget edited by David Elkind and John H. Flavell (New York: Oxford University Press, 1969). This anthology is primarily concerned with the investigations and theorizing of Piaget, whose work has inspired at least in part many of the recent developments.

Revolution in Learning: The Years from Birth to Six by Maya Pines (New York: Harper and Row, 1967). The nontechnical survey presented many of the developments in early childhood education before the investigators themselves had published their findings.

The Nature of Human Intelligence by J. P. Guilford (New York: McGraw Hill, 1967) describes the structure of intellect as this has been revealed by studies employing the method of factor analysis.

Experience, Structure, and Adaptability edited by O. J. Harvey (New York: Springer Publishing Co., 1966). This anthology includes a variety of investigations of the role of early experience in the development of flexibility and adaptability.

Intelligence and Experience by J. McV. Hunt (New York: Ronald Press, 1961). This heavily documented book describes in detail the evidence which is forcing a change in the conception of intelligence and of the degree of plasticity in early psychological development.

The Challenge of Incompetence and Poverty by J. McV. Hunt (Urbana: University of Illinois Press, 1969). This book, also well-documented, contains seven papers which describe the interconnection between poverty and lack of competence, gives the basis for preschool enrichment, and describes the results of the experimental attempts to intervene in the lives of the poor with preschool education and with parent education.

Intelligence — Why It Grows, Why It Declines

JOHN L. HORN

One of the oldest and most thoroughly studied concepts in psychology is the concept of intelligence. Yet the term "intelligence" still escapes precise definition. There are so many different kinds of behavior that are indicative of intelligence that identifying the essence of them all has seemed virtually impossible. However, some recent research indicates that much of the diversity seen in expressions of intelligence can be understood in terms of a relatively small number of concepts. What's more, this research has also given us insight into understanding where intelligence originates; how it develops; and why and when it increases or decreases.

Studies of the interrelationships among human abilities indicate that there are two basic types of intelligence: fluid intelligence and crystallized intelligence. Fluid intelligence is rather formless; it is relatively independent of education and experience; and it can "flow into" a wide variety of intellectual activities. Crystallized intelligence, on the other hand, is a precipitate out of experience. It results when fluid intelligence is "mixed" with what can be called "the intelligence of the culture." Crystallized intelligence increases with a person's experience, and with the education that provides new methods and perspectives for dealing with that experience.

These two major kinds of intelligence are composed of more elementary abilities, called "primary" mental abilities. The number of these primaries is small. Only about 30 can be accepted as really well established. But with just these 30 primaries, we can explain much of the person-to-person variation commonly observed in reasoning, thinking, problem-solving, inventing and understanding. Since several thousand tests have been devised to measure various aspects of intelligence, this system of primaries represents a very considerable achievement in parsimony. In much the same way that the chemical elements are organized according to the Periodic Law, these primary mental abilities fall into the patterns labeled fluid and crystallized intelligence.

What follows are some examples of the kinds of abilities that define fluid intelligence—and some of the tests that measure this kind of intelligence.

□ *Induction* is the ability to discover a general rule from several particular incidents and then apply this rule to cover a new incident.

For example, if a person observes the characteristics of a number of people who are members of a particular club or lodge, he might discover the rule by which membership is determined (even when this rule is highly secret information). He might then apply this rule to obtain an invitation to membership!

Among the tests that measure induction ability is the letter series. Given some letters in a series like
A C F J O —
the task is to provide the next letter. Of course, the test can be used only with people who know the alphabet, and this rules out illiterates and most children. We can't eliminate the influence of accumulated learning from even the purest examples of fluid intelligence.

☐ *Figural Relations* refers to the ability to notice changes or differences in shapes and use this awareness to identify or produce one element missing from a pattern.

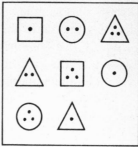

What figure fits into the lower right? (Answer: a square with two dots.)

An everyday example of intelligence in figural relations is the ability to navigate cloverleaf and expressway turnoff patterns—an ability that may mean as much for adequate adjustment today as skill in finding one's way through a virgin forest had in the days of Daniel Boone. This ability also has ready application in interior decorating and in jobs where maps (or aerial views) must be compared a good deal—as by cartographers, navigators, pilots, meteorologists and tourists.

☐ *Span of Apprehension* is the ability to recognize and retain awareness of the immediate environment. A simple test is memory span: Several digits or other symbols are presented briefly, and the task is to reproduce them later, perhaps in reverse order. Without this ability, remembering a telephone number long enough to dial it would be impossible.

Other primary abilities that help define fluid intelligence include:

☐ *General Reasoning* (example: estimating how long it would take to do several errands around town);

☐ *Semantic Relations* (example: enjoying a pun on common words);

☐ *Deductive Reasoning,* or the ability to reason from the general to the particular (example: noting that the wood of fallen trees rots and concluding that one should cover—for example, paint—wooden fence posts before inserting them into the ground);

☐ *Associative Memory*, or the ability to aid memory by observing the relationships between separate items (example: remembering the way to grandmother's house by associating various landmarks en route, or remembering the traits of different people by association with their faces).

Most of what we call intelligence—for example, the ability to make good use of language or to solve complex technical problems—is actually crystallized intelligence. Here are some of the primary abilities that demonstrate the nature of this kind of intelligence:

☐ *Verbal Comprehension.* This could also be called general information, since it represents a broad slice of knowledge. Vocabulary tests, current-events tests and reading-comprehension tests all measure verbal comprehension, as do other tests that require a person to recall information about his culture. The ability is rather fully exercised when one quickly reads an article like this one and grasps the essential ideas. Verbal comprehension is also called for when a person reads news items about foreign affairs, understands their implications, and relates them to one another and to their historical backgrounds.

□ *Experiential Evaluation* is often called "common sense" or "social intelligence." Experiential evaluation includes the ability to project oneself into situations, to feel as other people feel and thereby better understand interactions among people. Everyday examples include figuring out why a conscientious foreman is not getting good results from those under him, and why people disobey traffic laws more at some intersections than at others.

One test that measures experiential evaluation in married men is the following:

Your wife has just invested time, effort and money in a new hairdo. But it doesn't help her appearance at all. She wants your opinion. You should:

1. try to pretend that the hairdo is great;
2. state your opinion bluntly;
3. compliment her on her hairdo, but add minor qualifications; or,
4. refuse to comment.

Answer 3 is considered judged correct—on the grounds that husbands can't get away with answers 1 and 4, and answer 2 is likely to provoke undue strife.

□ *Formal Reasoning* is reasoning in ways that have become more or less formalized in Western cultures. An example is the syllogism, like this one:

No Gox box when in purple socks.

Jocks is a Gox wearing purple socks,

Therefore: Jocks does not now box.

The task is to determine whether or not the conclusion is warranted. (It is.)

An everyday example of formal reasoning might be to

produce a well-reasoned analysis of the pros and cons of an issue presented to the United Nations. Formal reasoning, to a much greater extent than experiential evaluation or verbal comprehension, depends upon dealing with abstractions and symbols in highly structured ways.

□ *Number Facility,* the primary ability to do numerical calculations, also helps define crystallized intelligence, since to a considerable extent it reflects the quality of a person's education. In a somewhat less direct way, this quality is also represented in the primary abilities called mechanical knowledge, judgment and associational fluency.

□ *Semantic Relations* and *General Reasoning,* listed as primary aspects of fluid intelligence, are also—when carrying a burden of learning and culture—aspects of crystallized intelligence. This points up the fact that, although fluid and crystallized intelligence represent distinct patterns of abilities, there is some overlap. This is what is known as *alternative mechanisms* in intellectual performance. In other words, a given kind of problem can sometimes be solved by exercise of different abilities.

Consider the general-reasoning primary, for example. In this, typical problems have a slightly mathematical flavor:

There are 100 patients in a hospital. Some (an even number) are one-legged, but wearing shoes. One-half of the remainder are barefooted. How many shoes are being worn?

We may solve this by using a formal algebraic equation. Set x equal to the number of one-legged patients, with 100-x then being the number of two--legged patients, and $x+\frac{1}{2}(100-x)2$ being the number of shoes worn. We don't have to invent the algebraic techniques used here. They have been passed down to us over centuries. As Keith Hayes very nicely puts it, "The culture relieves us of much of the burden of creativity by giving us access to the products of creative acts scattered thinly through the history of the species." The use of such products is an important part of crystallized intelligence.

But this problem can also be solved by a young boy who has never heard of algebra! He may reason that, if half the two-legged people are without shoes, and all the rest (an even number) are one-legged, then the shoes must average one per person, and the answer must be 100. This response, too, represents learning—but it is not so much a product of education, or of the accumulated wisdom passed from one generation to the next, as is the typical product of crystallized intelligence. Fluid intelligence is composed of such relatively untutored skills.

Thus the same problem can be solved by exercise of *either* fluid intelligence *or* crystallized intelligence. We can also see the operation of such alternative mechanisms in these two problems.

ZEUS–JUPITER: ARTEMIS–?

Answer: Phidias Coria *Diana*

HERE–NOW: THERE–?

Answer: Thus Sometimes *Then*

The first problem is no harder to solve than the second, *provided* you have acquired a rather sophisticated knowledge of mythology. The second problem requires learning too, but no more than simply learning the language—a fact that puts native-born whites and Negroes on a relatively equal footing in dealing with problems of this sort, but places Spanish-speaking Puerto Ricans or Mexican-Americans at a disadvantage. As measures of fluid intelligence, both items are about equally good. But the first involves, to a much greater extent, crystallized intelligence gleaned from formal education or leisure reading.

Because the use of alternative mechanisms is natural in the play of human intelligence, most intelligence tests provide mixed rather than pure measures of fluid or crystallized abilities. This only reflects the way in which we usually go about solving problems—by a combination of natural wit and acquired strategies. But tests can be devised in which one type of intelligence predominates. For example, efforts to devise "culture fair" intelligence tests that won't discriminate against people from deprived educational or cultural backgrounds usually focus on holding constant the effect of crystallized capabilities—so that fluid capabilities can be more fully represented.

Now that we have roughly defined what fluid and crystallized intelligence are, let us investigate how each of them develops over time.

The infant, whose reasoning powers extend little beyond the observation that a determined howl brings food, attention or a dry diaper, becomes the man who can solve legal problems all day, execute complicated detours to avoid the five o'clock traffic on his way home and deliver a rousing speech to his political club in the evening. But how? To understand the intertwined development of the fluid and crystallized abilities that such activities require, we need to consider three processes essential to the development of intelligence: anlage function, the acquisition of aids and concept formation.

Anlage function, which includes the complex work-
ings of the brain and other nervous tissue, provides the
physical base for all of the infant's future mental
growth. ("Anlage" is a German word meaning "rudi-
ment.") The second two factors—the aids and concepts
the child acquires as he grows up—represent the building
blocks that, placed on the anlage base, form the
structure of adult intelligence.

The anlage function depends crucially and directly
upon physiology. Physiology, in turn, depends partly on
heredity, but it can also be influenced by injury, disease,
poisons, drugs and severe shocks. Such influences can
occur very early in life—often even in the womb. Hence
it is quite possible that an individual's anlage functioning may have only a remote relationship to his hereditary potential. All we can say for sure is that the anlage
process *is* closely tied to a physiological base.

A good everyday measure of a person's anlage
functioning is his memory span (provided we can rule
out the effects of anxiety, fatigue or mental disturbance). Given a series of letters or numbers, most adults
can immediately reproduce only about six or seven of
them in reverse order. Some people may be able to
remember 11, others as few as four, but in no case is the
capacity unlimited or even very great. Memory span
increases through childhood—probably on account of
the increasing size and complexity of the brain—but it is
not much affected by learning. This is generally true of
other examples of anlage functioning.

Aids are techniques that enable us to go beyond the
limitations imposed by anlage functioning. An aid can,
for example, extend our memory span. For example, we
break up a telephone or social-security number with
dashes, transforming long numbers into short, more

easily recalled sets, and this takes the strain off immediate memory.

Some aids, like the rules of algebra, are taught in school. But several psychologists (notably Jean Piaget) have demonstrated that infants and children also invent their own aids in their untutored explorations of the world. In development, this process probably continues for several years.

Concepts are categories we impose on the phenomena we experience. In forming concepts, we find that otherwise dissimilar things can be regarded as "the same" in some sense because they have common properties. For instance, children learn to distinguish the features associated with "bike"—two wheels, pedaling, riding outside, etc.—from those associated with "car." Very early in a child's development, these categories may be known and represented only in terms of his own internal symbols. In time, however, the child learns to associate his personal symbols with conventional signs—that is, he learns to use language to represent what he "knows" from direct experience. Also, increased proficiency in the use of language affords opportunities to see new relations and acquire new concepts.

The concepts we possess at any time are a residue of previous intellectual functioning. Tests that indicate the extent of this residue may, therefore, predict the level of a person's future intellectual development. A large vocabulary indicates a large storehouse of previously acquired concepts, so verbal ability itself is often taken as a good indication of ability to conceptualize. Many well-known tests of intelligence, especially of crystallized intelligence, are based on this rationale.

However, language is really only an indirect measure

of concept awareness. Thus verbally oriented tests can be misleading. What about the child raised in an environment where language is seldom used, but which is otherwise rich in opportunity to perceive relationships and acquire concepts (the backwoods of Illinois, or by a pond in Massachusetts)? At the extreme, what about a person who never hears the spoken word or sees the written word? He does not necessarily lack the awareness that we so glibly represent in language. Nor does he necessarily lack intelligence. A child who doesn't know the spoken or written word "key" surely understands the concept if he can distinguish a key from other small objects and use it to open a lock.

What is true of conventional language is also true of conventional aids. Lack of facility or familiarity with aids does not mean that a child has failed to develop intellectually, even though it may make him appear mentally slow on standard intelligence tests. Just as verbally oriented tests penalize the child who has not had the formal schooling or proper environment to develop a large vocabulary, many tests of so-called mathematical aptitude rely heavily on the use of conventional aids taught in school—on algebraic formulas, for example. Someone who has learned few of these conventional aids will generally do poorly on such tests, but this does not mean that he lacks intelligence.

We cannot overlook the fact that an intelligent woodsman may be just as intelligent, in one sense of this term, as an intelligent college professor. The particular combination of primary abilities needed to perform well may differ in the two cases, but the basic wherewithal of intellectual competence can be the same—adequate anlage functioning, plus an awareness of the concepts and a facility with the aids relevant to dealing with the environment at hand. Daniel Boone surely needed as much intelligence to chart the unexplored forests of the frontier as today's professor needs to thread his way through the groves of academe.

It is obvious, then, that formal education is not essential to the development of important aspects of intelligence. Barring disruption of anlage functioning by accident or illness, the child will form concepts and devise aids to progressively expand his mental grasp as he grows up, and this will occur whether he goes to school or not.

Where formal instruction *is* significant is in making such development easier—and in passing along the concepts and aids that many people have deposited into the intelligence of a culture. The schools give children awareness of concepts that they may not have had the opportunity to gain from first-hand experience—the ability to recognize an Australian platypus, for example, without ever having seen one, or a knowledge of how the caste system works in India. Aids, too, are taught in school. A child well-armed with an array of mathematical formulas will likely be able to solve a problem faster and more accurately than one who must work it out completely on his own. Indeed, some problems simply cannot be solved without mathematical aids. Since the acquisition of both concepts and aids is cumulative, several years of formal education can put one child well ahead of another one, unschooled, who has roughly the same intellectual potential.

Education can thus play a powerful role in developing intelligence. Too often, however, it doesn't. Even in school, some children in perfectly good health and physical condition fail to develop, or develop slowly. Some even seem to be mentally stunted by their school

experience. Why? What sorts of experiences can foster—
or retard—the developmental processes of concept-
formation and aid-formation in the school environment?

Even though we are only beginning to find answers in
this area, it is already clear that learning can be speeded
up, slowed down or brought almost to a dead halt by a
variety of school experiences. On the favorable side,
abilities improve by *positive transfer*. Learning one skill
makes it easier to learn a related one. A student who
already knows Spanish, for example, will find it easier
to learn Portuguese. And positive transfer also works in
less obvious ways. There is even evidence to suggest that
new learning is facilitated simply by having learned
before—by a sort of learning how to learn.

But other factors too can affect the course of
learning, and these factors are particularly prominent in
the context of our formal educational system. For
example, merely having the opportunity to learn may
depend on both previous learning and previous opportunity to learn. Thus, even if his native potential and
level of self-education are good, the person who has not
had the opportunity to finish high school has a poor
chance of going on to college.

Labeling operates in a similar way. If a person is
labeled as lacking in ability, he may receive no further
chance to develop. Kenneth B. Clark states this very
well:

> If a child scores low on an intelligence test because he
> cannot read and then is not taught to read because he
> has a low score, then such a child is being imprisoned
> in an *iron circle* and becomes the victim of an
> educational self-fulfilling prophecy.

Avoidance-learning is similar. This is learning not to
learn. Punishment in a learning situation—being humili-

ated in school, for example—may make a child "turn
off." Problem-solving may become such a threat that he
will avoid all suggestion of it. Since an active, inquiring
curiosity is at the root of mental growth, avoidance-
learning can very seriously retard intellectual development. Moreover, since a child typically expresses avoid-
ance by aggression, lack of attention, sullenness and
other behavior unacceptable to educators and parents,
they—being human—may react by shutting the child out
of further learning situations, and thus create another
kind of iron circle.

Labeling, lack of opportunity, and avoidance-learning
affect the development of both fluid and crystallized
intelligence. Both depend upon acculturational
influences—the various factors that provide, or block,
chances for learning. And both depend upon anlage
function and thus upon physiological influences as well.
However, fluid intelligence depends more on physiological factors, and crystallized intelligence more on
acculturational ones. It is the interplay of these factors
throughout a child's development that produces the fact
that fluid and crystallized intelligence can be separated
in adult intellectual performances. But how does this
separation arise?

In many respects, the opportunities to maintain good
physiological health are the same for all in our society.
The climate, air pollution, water, the chances of injury
and other hazards in the physical environment do not
vary greatly. Even the social environments are similar in
many ways. We acquire similar language skills, go to
schools that have similar curricula, have a similar choice
of television programs and so on. In this sense, the most
advantaged and the most disadvantaged child have some

of the same opportunities to develop anlage functioning, and to acquire concepts and aids.

Moreover, we should be careful about how we use the term "disadvantaged." We do not yet know what is superior in all respects, at every age level, for the development of all the abilities that go into intelligence. At one stage, what seems a "bad" home may give intelligence a greater impetus than an apparently "good" home. It may be, for instance, that in early childhood "lax" parents allow more scope for development. In later development, "stimulating" and "responsible" (but restrictive?) parents might be better. Some of the intellectual leaders of every period of history and of every culture have developed in environments that, according to many definitions, would have to be classified as "disadvantaged."

It is clear, however, that favorable conditions for the development of intelligence are not the same for all. To avoid the iron circle, to gain opportunities to go on, children have to display the right abilities at the right times. To some extent, this depends on early and basic endowment. Intelligent parents may provide good heredity, good environmental conditions for learning and good stimulation and encouragement. But the opportunities a child gets, and what he meets them with, can also be quite independent of his own characteristics. His opportunities depend on such haphazard factors as the neighborhood in which he lives, the kind of schooling available, his mother's interests and his father's income, the personality qualities of the teachers he happens to get, and the attitudes and actions of his playmates.

Thus, through a child's years of growth and education, societal influences can produce an effect that is

largely independent of those produced by physiological
influences. In an infant, cultural influences could not
have accumulated independently of the physiological.
But as children pass through preschool and school, their
awareness of concepts and use of aids becomes more
evident, and the influence of acculturation is felt and
exhibited. The probable shape of future learning and
opportunity becomes more clear. The child who has
already moved ahead tends to be ready to move farther
ahead, and to be accepted for such promotion. Crystallized intelligence feeds the growth of crystallized intelligence. By contrast, the child who has not moved ahead,
for whatever reasons, tends to be less ready and to be
viewed as such. His acquisition of the lore of the culture
proceeds at a decelerating rate. This is how two children
with roughly the same hereditary potential can grow
apart in their acquisition of crystallized intelligence.
Among adults, then, we should expect to find great
variation in the crystallized pattern of abilities—and we
do!

The cultural influences that can produce this kind of
inequality operate almost independently of physiological factors, however. Thus, the child who fails to
progress rapidly in learning the ever-more-abstruse concepts and aids of crystallized intelligence may still
acquire many concepts and aids of a more common
type. And if he is lucky in avoiding accidents and
maintaining good health, this kind of development can
be quite impressive. His intellectual growth may even
surpass that of a seemingly more favored child who is
slowed down by illness or injury. Thus, two children
with about the same hereditary makeup can grow apart
in fluid intelligence, too. The result is a wide range of
variation in adult fluid intelligence—a range even wider

than we would expect to be produced by differences in heredity alone.

Both fluid and crystallized intelligence, as we have just seen, develop with age. But intelligence also declines with age. This is especially true of the fluid kind. Looked at in terms of averages, fluid intelligence begins to decline before a person is out of his 20s. Crystallized intelligence fares better, however, and generally continues to increase throughout life. Because crystallized intelligence usually increases in this fashion, the decline in fluid abilities may not seriously undermine intellectual competence in people as they mature into middle age and even beyond. But let us look at these matters more analytically.

The graph below represents results from several studies, each involving several hundred people. Notice, first, that the curves representing fluid intelligence (FI) and crystallized intelligence (CI) are at first indis-

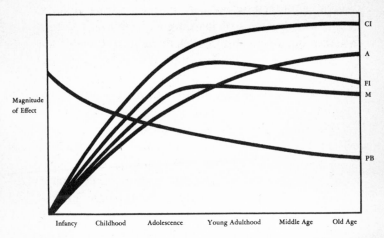

Development of Fluid Intelligence (FI) and
Crystallized Intelligence (CI) in relation to effects produced by Maturation (M),
Acculturation (A), and loss of Physiological Base (PB) due to injury.

tinguishable, but become separate as development proceeds. This represents the fact that both are products of
development. It also illustrates the fact that it is easier
to distinguish between fluid intelligence and crystallized
intelligence in adults than in children.

The maturation curve (M) summarizes evidence that
the physical structures and processes that support
intellect (the brain, for instance) grow and increase in
complexity until the late teens or the early 20s.
Development is rapid but decelerating. Since both fluid
and crystallized intelligence depend on maturation, their
curves more or less follow it.

But maturation accounts for only part of the change
in the physical structures that support intelligence. They
are also affected by injuries, such as birth complications,
blows to the head, carbon-monoxide poisoning, intoxi-
cation and high fever. Such injuries are irreversible and
thus cumulative. In the short run, they are difficult to
discern, and their effects are masked during childhood
by the rising curves of learning and maturation. In the
long run, however, injuries resulting from the exposures
of living take their toll. The older the person, the greater
the exposure. Thus, part of the physiological base for
intellectual functioning will, on an average decrease with
age (curve PB).

The sum of the influences represented by M and PB
form the physiological base for intellectual processes at
any particular time. In the early years, the effects of one
compensate for the effects of the other. But as the M
curve levels off in young adulthood and the PB curve
continues downward, the total physiological base drops.
Those intellectual abilities that depend very directly
upon physiology must then decline.

The effects of brain-tissue loss are variable, however.

At the physiological level, an ability is a complex network of neurons that "fire" together to produce observable patterns of behavior. Such networks are overdetermined—not all of the neurons in the network need to "fire" to produce the behavior. And some networks are much more overdetermined than others. This means that when a loss of brain tissue (that is, a loss of neurons) occurs, some networks, and hence some abilities, will be only minimally affected. Networks that are not highly overdetermined, though, will become completely inoperative when a critical number of neurons cease to fire.

The crystallized abilities apparently correspond to highly overdetermined neural networks. Such abilities will not be greatly affected by moderate loss of neurons. The fluid abilities, on the other hand, depend much more significantly upon anlage functions, which are represented by very elementary neural networks. These abilities will thus "fall off" with a loss of neurons.

Curve A in the graph shows how, potentially at least, the effects of acculturation and positive transfer may accumulate throughout a lifetime. On this basis alone, were it not for neural damage, we might expect intelligence to increase, not decline, in adulthood.

Whether intellectual decline occurs or not will depend upon the extent of neuron loss, and upon whether learning new aids and concepts can compensate for losing old skills. For example, the anlage capacity to keep six digits in immediate awareness may decline with loss of neurons. But the individual, sensing this loss, may develop new techniques to help him keep a number in mind. Thus the overall effect may be no loss of ability. What the evidence does indicate, however, is that, with increasing age beyond the teens, there is a steady, if gentle, decline in fluid intelligence. This suggests that learning new aids and concepts of the fluid kind does not quite compensate for the loss of anlage function and the loss of previously learned aids and concepts.

On a happier note, and by way of contrast, the evidence also shows that crystallized intelligence *increases* throughout most of adulthood. Here alternative mechanisms come into play. Compensating for the loss of one ability with the surplus of another, the older person uses crystallized intelligence in place of fluid intelligence. He substitutes accumulated wisdom for brilliance, while the younger person does the opposite.

A word of caution about these results. They represent averages, and averages can be affected by a relatively few extreme cases. For example, if only a relatively few individuals experience brain damage, but the effect is rather pronounced in each case, this will show up in the averages. If such damage occurs more frequently with older people than with younger people, a corresponding decline of abilities with age will show up—even though such decline may not be an inevitable aspect of aging for everyone. But even though these cautions must be kept in mind, we should not lose track of the fact that the FI curve parallels the PB in adulthood.

Intelligence tests that measure mixtures of fluid and crystallized intelligence (and most popular ones do) show varying relationships between aging and intelligence in adulthood. If fluid tests predominate, decline is indicated. If crystallized intelligence is well represented, then there is no apparent decline.

Intellectual performance in important jobs in life will depend on both kinds of intelligence, and may be represented by a composite curve (FI and CI in the

graph below). Notice that the peak of this curve occurs
later than the peak of the FI curve below it. If fluid
intelligence reaches its peak in the early 20s, intelligence
in overall performance, influenced by the cultural
accretion, may peak in the 30s. The evidence indicates
that the greatest intellectual *productivity* tends to occur
in the 30s or early 40s, although the most *creative* work
often is accomplished earlier. For example, half of the
52 greatest discoveries in chemistry (as judged by
chemists) were made before the innovator had reached
age 29, and 62 percent were made before he was 40. It

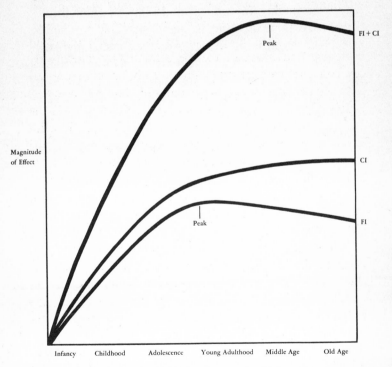

Fluid intelligence, crystallized intelligence,
and the effect of the two added together.

would seem that creativity and productivity represent somewhat different combinations of fluid and crystallized intelligence, with productivity being relatively more affected by cultural factors.

The age at which the combined FI and CI function peaks varies from one person to another, depending on the development of new concepts and aids, the amount of brain damage, and other factors such as diet and general health.

Perhaps the most interesting result of all this recent work lies in the questions it provokes. What are the factors producing the apparent decline in fluid intelligence? Are they intrinsic to aging, or do they merely reflect the hazards of living? Are they associated with the hazards of different occupations? Do auto mechanics, for example, who are repeatedly exposed to carbon monoxide, show more decline in fluid intelligence than cement finishers, who work in the open air?

Most important of all, what experiences in infancy and childhood have favorable or unfavorable effects on the future growth of fluid intelligence? Of crystallized intelligence? Of both? Do experiences that affect fluid intelligence always affect crystallized intelligence, too? We are still far from finding firm and comprehensive answers to these questions, but they very clearly hold massive implications for our child-rearing practices, for our educational system and for the whole complex of fields that bear on the development and management of human potential.

November 1967

OF SOCIAL CLASS
AND EDUCATION

Part II.

The Demographic Context
of Metropolitan Education

KARL E. TAEUBER

The American educational system is beset with anachronisms. Like the American political system and many associated administrative systems the educational system splits the nation into states, states into districts, and districts into neighborhoods. Implicit in this scheme is an ideological romanticism, harking back to the good old rural past when the countryside was dotted with villages each of which linked the surrounding farm families to a core of community institutions and services. Add to the picture a New England town meeting, and you have the prototype of rural American democracy.

Twentieth-century events have made the preceding picture impractical for an understanding of present-day educational problems. Instead we need a geography that considers the relationship of populations to populations: that discusses urbanization and suburbanization;

migration and population movement within urban areas, and the resulting age patterns and numbers of school age children; and racial residential segregation and its relationship to school segregation. In this chapter I shall attempt to outline the ways in which such geographic analyses might be made.

Urbanization and Suburbanization

Imagine an ordinary relief map of the United States. A mountain peak projecting 10,000 feet above the surface of the earth is represented on the map by a peak of one or two inches. Now, redraw the map, letting height represent the number of people per square mile. In this new map, both Death Valley and the Rocky Mountains are represented as valleys. Various coastal locations, virtually at sea level, are sites of enormous peaks. The entire map is a series of greater and lesser peaks, with steep slopes and highly variegated plateaus separating the peaks.

If a series of our special relief maps were constructed, one for each census date, we could visualize the process of urbanization of the United States. At the first census in 1790 there would be an eastern plateau, sloping off to the west, representing the inhabited portion of the new nation. The plateau would be studded with small peaks. Even the few large peaks would be smaller than dozens of those on the 1960 map. Let us jump to 1910. Not only had the number and size of urban peaks greatly increased, but the farm population was more numerous than before or since. In recent decades, most counties in the nation have lost population; the general level of the plateau was lower in 1960 than in 1910. There were more high peaks, and many of the high ones had become much broader or fatter. In fact, for a number of the highest ones the principal change in recent years has been an increase in breadth rather than height.

The principal topographic features of our map are the mountains, the metropolitan areas. But although the peaks are clearly distinguishable, it is not clear precisely where the base of each peak ends and where the next begins. This is particularly true of certain sectors: the northeastern seaboard, for example, or along the southern edge of the Great Lakes.

The federal government has developed a compromise solution to this problem, at least for purposes of data-gathering. This approach, used since the 1950 census, merges our relief map with the standard political map. Mixing practicality and scholarly idealism, counties are taken as the building blocks. Around each large city (each nodal point on our map) a metropolitan area is defined, consisting of the county containing the city and, if appropriate, contiguous counties which (according to patterns of commuting, telephone calls and the like) are socially and economically integrated with the city.

From 1910 to 1970 "metropolitan mountains" pushed upward all over the map. By 1970 two-thirds of the United States population was metropolitan. This metropolitan concentration embraces both races; indeed, the nationwide figure for Negroes is now a bit higher than that for whites, even though in some Southern areas the Negro population has grown more slowly than the white population.

Where has the added population been housed? The principal source of additional housing is new construction. (Subdivision of existing units was prevalent during the tight housing market of the 1940s, but is inherently limited in magnitude.) Given the market system that prevails in the United States, new housing tends to be moderately expensive. It has tended to be single-family units, owner occupied, with a private yard. This housing pattern gobbles up space, and space has been available mainly at the edges of the built-up area. In the past, cities tended to annex areas as they were initially built up and occupied. Hence the growth of the expanding metropolis was in large part contained within the growth of the city. During the last 50 years, however, annexation has become much less frequent, and much metropolitan growth occurs outside city limits. In great measure, therefore, the much-ballyhooed process of suburbanization is simply the old process of urbanization. The difference is largely the differential use of the political annexation process rather than a fundamental change in the process of metropolitan expansion. Suburbanization is simply the continued outward growth of the metropolis.

This view of suburbanization does not deny the very real differences between middle-class suburb and lower-class ghetto. With respect to types of housing, these differences reflect not so much differences between suburbanization and urbanization as between urbanization in the 1880s and urbanization in the 1950s and 1960s. Changing consumer preferences together with changes in technology, financing and organization of the construction industry have led to major changes in styles of housing. Rather than compare single-family home with tenement, it suffices to compare current central-city high-density apartment developments with old tenement patterns, or new suburban homes with old. Changes in settlement patterns result also from the larger number of families with more real income.

Widespread automobile ownership and freeway construction have permitted new housing to spread over the landscape rather than concentrate along mass transportation routes.

Many central cities are now losing population while the suburbs continue to grow rapidly. This loss of central city population need not be taken as a radical sign of urban decay. It is more appropriate to envision every neighborhood as having a normal life cycle. An area is likely to be platted and opened to residential development as the transportation of the era—rail or surface—makes the location accessible and as other sites more attractive by contemporary standards are occupied. (The relevant measures of attractiveness of an area are not only the whims of potential residents but also the views of potential builders who are subject to numerous technological and financial constraints.) At first the housing is new, but the passage of time wreaks a toll in two ways. Housing which was new and up-to-date very soon lags behind newer housing in fashion and technological convenience. In addition, maintenance costs increase with the passage of time, both from aging of the building and from rising costs of labor. In some neighborhoods the residents or owners have the inclination and the resources continually to maintain and upgrade the housing; in others they do not.

Typically, the initial period of settlement is followed by a period of consolidation, as the remaining vacant lots are occupied and other opportunities to add to the housing supply are utilized. After a period of relative stability, the neighborhood may begin to decline in its attractiveness to the kind of residents originally there. This may lead to substantial conversion to a denser

residential pattern, but in the long run it leads to an
absolute decline in marketability, to high vacancy rates,
to displacement for urban renewal or highway construction, and to declining population.

The two world wars and the great depression were
periods of little home construction. The 1920s, 1950s
and 1960s were periods of rapid home construction. But
they were also periods of rapid population growth and
new household formation. In many metropolitan areas,
much of the total housing stock antedates the first
world war. This is particularly true of housing within
city limits, the more so if those limits were expanded
around the turn of the century to embrace most of the
built-up area but have changed little since. With a slow
rate of replacement of existing housing, this old housing
is very old indeed. The decline in city populations
reflects a decline in use of this ancient housing. It
contributes to the improvement of the housing of the
bulk of the population, and from this perspective is a
cause for celebration rather than despair. To be sure
declining city populations create problems, but these
take a far different shape from a national or even a
metropolitan perspective than they do from the vantage
point of a mayor's office or a board of education.

I shall return to the topic of city-suburban differences, but I'd like to approach it in terms of processes
rather than as a static picture. Hence it will be necessary
first to talk a bit about the process of migration—people
moving from one place to another, from farm to city,
from city to suburb, from suburb to city and so forth.

Patterns of Migration

When the oldest members of our population were
born, the nation was predominantly rural. Already,

however, we were in the midst of rapid urbanization based on our own rural surplus and on the immigration of millions of Europeans. Today we are a nation of cities, and the predominant pattern of movement is from city to city. The farm population continues to send migrants to cities, but the numbers involved are small and growing smaller. In the contemporary scene, the new migrant that attracts the attention of welfare agencies and reformers is not the foreigner or the Okie but the rural Negro. I shall begin with a discussion of Negro migration and then move to a separate discussion of white migration and suburbanization.

Most southern cities have always had a sizeable representation of Negroes in the population, but for many northern cities the period from about 1919 to 1925 produced the first large influx of Negro population. The fragmentary sources upon which we base most of what is known about the early period of large-scale Negro migration are in general agreement that Negro in-migrants to cities were of lower social and economic status than the resident Negro and white populations. Increased racial tensions were blamed upon the heavy influx of Negroes of low socioeconomic status. Even the old Negro residents are reported to have shared in resentment of the new in-migrants:

> Inevitably many of them were inclined to hold the migrants responsible for these increasing social restrictions and tended to resent the influx of other blacks, many of whom were inferior in education and culture to the northern Negroes and many of whom were unaccustomed to northern standards of living and modes of conduct.

This early migration was brought to a halt by economic crisis and the depression. Migration resumed with the industrial boom of the early 1940s. Through the late 1940s and early 1950s there was a continued shift of Negroes from the rural South to the urban North and South. An extensive literature, both popular and scholarly, paints and repaints the same picture that was painted in 1917 and 1927. Whites are presumed to be abandoning cities to a Negro population increasing daily through the addition of low-status migrants who burden schools, welfare agencies, police and other public agencies. The extreme portrait in this painting is that of the urban newcomer so unsophisticated in the mysteries of urban life that he throws his garbage out the window unaware that no pigs feed in the alley below. I'm sure that welfare workers and teachers have encountered occasional families of this type, and in that sense there is the inevitable kernel of truth to the picture. But the degree of truth is less than in the typical racial stereotype. A study of the characteristics of the in-migrants and their growth replaces the stereotype with a picture of men and women working hard to achieve a better life for themselves and their children.

First I wish to emphasize that massive migrations are necessarily limited in duration. A shift from migration to natural increase as the principal source of growth is typical for migrant populations. After an early period of migration, the resident population is large enough to produce a significant natural increase. As the resident base increases, a steady rate of migration produces a smaller and smaller relative rate of growth. This shift is augmented by the tendency for migrants to be concentrated in the young adult ages, so that family formation is rapid and birth rates are high. It is also quite natural for the migration itself to diminish. Although in many northern cities the volume of Negro in-migration has continued to be high its character has changed and its proportionate share of metropolitan growth has declined. There are hardly any more Negro sharecroppers; the rural Negro population has been declining; and there is an increasing number of cities in both North and South to which Negroes now move.

Many discussions of migration rely, most unfortunately, on data on *net* migration. A net migration of 10,000 may result from an in-migration of 10,000 and an out-migration of zero, or from a in-migration of 100,000 and an out-migration of 90,000. Knowing the net balance really tells us very little about migration. Furthermore, we are usually interested in the characteristics of the migrants, and this makes it necessary to identify individual migrants. After all, there is no such creature as a "net migrant." Without a population register identification of migrants requires surveys. We can learn much from the largest survey of all, the decennial census. The relevant 1970 census results are not yet available. In the 1960 census each person in a sample was asked where he lived five years before. If not at the same address, he was classified as a local-mover if still in the same city, or as a migrant if he had moved from elsewhere. Census data for the period 1955-60 reveal the following features of Negro migration to northern and border cities:

Contrary to the popular stereotype, Negro in-migrants . . . were not of lower average socio-economic status than the resident Negro population. Indeed, in educational attainment Negro in-migrants . . . were equal to or slightly higher than the resident white population. Comparisons with limited data for earlier periods suggest that, as the Negro population has changed from a disadvantaged rural population to a metropolitan one of increasing socioeconomic levels, its patterns of migration have changed to become very much like those of the white population.

A portion of the Negro migrants to each city formerly lived in the nonmetropolitan South. This portion tends to be of low socioeconomic status, though not as low as the stereotype suggests. The significant unrecognized factor is that this portion is relatively small compared to the total volume of migration. There is much movement of Negroes from city to city within the North, and from southern cities to northern cities. It takes a person with at least a modicum of ambition, money and knowledge of opportunities at the destination to move a long distance to a radically new type of job and community. Hence, long-distance migration tends to be selective of the more successful rather than the less successful.

Long-distance migration is not the only option available to a Negro farm-laborer dispossessed by a new minimum wage law or to a Negro teenager who knows rural life isn't for him. There is probably a nearby town or city to which relatives and friends have gone, which he has visited previously, and which offers an easier refuge than the big city up North. Each southern metropolis carries on an exchange of poorly educated, unskilled Negroes with an extensive rural hinterland. The flow is both ways, and by now there are few rural people so isolated as to have no meaningful contacts with the urban way of life.

In 1885, a Britisher named Ravenstein published an article on "The Laws of Migration." His laws are really generalizations based on his study of the limited migration data then available for a few countries, but they have stood the test of time and hold up remarkably well in other places at other times. One of these laws is that most migrants are young adults. It is youth who lead the redistribution of population, who abandon old ways of life and try out the new. In recent decades in the United States, even in the rural South, nearly all children attended school, and through time there has been a tendency for the amount of schooling to increase. Hence, each new generation of youthful migrants is better educated than the last. Not only does long-distance migration tend to select the better educated, but it selects from among the best-educated age group in society.

A second of Ravenstein's laws concerns the prevalence of stage migration. Although we talk of the shift of people from farms to giant cities, actual movements tend to be in stages, with farm-reared youth moving to towns, town-reared youth moving to the nearest city, and city-reared youth moving to more distant cities. Despite spectacular examples of direct migration from backwoods farm to modern metropolis, there is much evidence that stage migration is the more typical pattern. People change their life styles gradually, and the migrant to St. Louis or Chicago who has never before seen a large city is a rare individual, no matter how dramatic his personal situation.

A generalization that emerges from the preceding but does not have the universality of Ravenstein's law is that selective migration can lower the status of both the sending and receiving populations. Rural counties that lose all of their Negro grade school graduates to the nearby cities have their average educational level lowered. But these migrants may be poorly educated by the standards of urban Negroes, thus lowering the average educational level of the city. Similarly, many of the urban southern Negroes who move to the urban North are well educated by the standards of their home communities, but not so by the standards prevailing in the northern cities. This paradox points to the community problems created by migration patterns which, on an individual level, may be highly beneficial.

The redistribution of white population has obeyed the same general "laws." I shall skip over the massive rural to urban migration of whites, and only briefly summarize a study of white migration between cities and suburbs.

Within the twelve largest metropolitan areas, there has been a substantial flow of persons in both directions—from city to suburb and from suburb to city. Indeed, Ravenstein once again hit the mark by postulating that each principal current of migration generates a countercurrent. Hence, there has long been a "back-to-the-city" movement, which accounts for the ease with which Sunday supplements find cases to illustrate that the central city is attracting back those frustrated suburbanites. Of course cities attract some suburbanites. But cities continue to lose to suburbs faster than they gain back. In this circulation of migrants, the general socioeconomic status tends to be higher than for nonmigrants. The principal migrants are single men and women and young families. They seek new housing not so much for status as for the space and style they always wanted but couldn't afford or which they could get along without because their kids were small.

Some metropolitan migrants are of low economic status. They are likely to find housing in older neighborhoods and hence in the central city. Migrants of higher status are likely to seek newer housing, and hence to locate in the suburbs. Persons of really low status are unlikely to do much moving except between apartments within a neighborhood. The problem of city poverty and suburban wealth is only in small part a result of poor people flooding into the cities and rich people moving out. Rather, large cities contribute to suburbs and to other metropolitan areas more high-status migrants than they receive, whereas suburban rings receive more high-status migrants than they lose. The net effect of this circulation is to diminish the socioeconomic level of central city populations and augment the socio-economic level of suburban populations. The process of population redistribution within the metropolis is much more complicated than public discussion would suggest.

The analyses underlying the preceding discussion of migration have concentrated on large cities. Current evidence suggests that newer and smaller cities are heading in the direction of these older and larger places, but they have not all reached the same point. In many of these places, the suburban populations are not superior to city populations in average levels of educa-tion, occupation or income. Even where the average levels are in the expected direction of higher suburban status, the magnitude of the difference is small. There are college graduates in the cities and high school dropouts in the suburbs.

Many persons read popular essays on suburbia and forget their own observations. Many delightful suburban-type areas lie within city limits, and many places outside city limits are really slums. Suburban squalor in the South is obvious in the rural villages and enclaves of shacks that have been brought into the urban sphere by its outward growth. We are so accustomed to a mental picture of suburbia that we tend to feel that these are nonsuburban places. If the definition of suburbs is restricted to certain "nice" residential neighborhoods, it is still obvious that suburbs may be found in the city as well as outside. The number and size of such neighborhoods are nowhere near as great as the simple city-suburb population figures would suggest. Carefully zoned half-acre developments impress us, and lead us to ignore the much greater number of families housed in denser and less luxurious settlement patterns.

Differences between cities and suburbs are more often exaggerated than minimized. My effort here is not to deny differences, but to call attention to similarities. The U.S. Commission on Civil Rights in its recent report on school segregation noted that 55 percent of college graduates in metropolitan areas live in suburbs contrasted with 55 percent of those without a high school diploma living in central cities. The figures may be presumed correct, but for present purposes I would turn them around to change the emphasis: 45 percent of metropolitan college graduates live in central cities, while 45 percent of the poorly educated live in suburbs. Central cities are not lacking in middle-class residents, nor are suburbs lacking in working-class residents.

Changing Age Composition

I studied the changes 1950-60 for the aggregate population of the 24 largest metropolitan areas, and have checked preliminary 1970 census results to be sure the major patterns still obtain. Obviously such an aggregate does not perfectly represent any one area, but the pattern is typical of most large and many small metropolitan areas. It only takes a glance to see the paucity of suburban nonwhites. Although the suburban nonwhite population increased in every age group, the numbers involved are small. The large percentage increases sometimes cited to prove that Negroes are suburbanizing are clearly misleading if not put in the context of the small numbers.

In the absence of suburbanization, the white population in central cities should have increased at most ages. In fact, there were only small increases at the main school ages, and very large decreases at ages 20-29. The suburbs showed tremendous gains in numbers of school-age whites.

The patterns become more complex when the city and suburban figures for whites and nonwhites are examined for specific age groups in specific areas. The data cannot be interpreted sensibly without keeping in mind the way in which they are affected by national fertility trends. For the total United States, the number of people in a given age group depends mainly on the number of births during the approporate earlier period. For more than a decade, the United States has had about 3,500,000 births a year, and this has led to a national stability in the numbers entering each elementary grade each year. But as the baby-boom children form families of their own, these numbers will increase even if birth rates decline. Hence, new fluctuating waves will eventually be rippling through the school systems. At the local level, migration patterns may augment the national waves, or produce counter currents.

Projections of school enrollment are very difficult, as many school administrators have learned through bitter experience. It is possible to keep track of the national demographic waves, and to anticipate their impact. It is harder, but not impossible, to project past suburbanization trends into the future. The census data cited earlier indicate that metropolitan population is still growing, that this growth is mainly in the suburbs, and that the suburbs remain largely closed to Negroes. Another complication is the existence of private school systems alongside the public system. Negroes make up a much greater percentage of public than of private school enrollment. Rarely do private school systems have a large percentage enrollment of Negroes. Suburban private schools typically have only a token Negro enrollment, and even suburban public schools confront a small Negro enrollment. With some exceptions, it is the public school systems in central cities that have large Negro enrollments, and it is only for these school systems that it is inherently difficult even to design a desegregation program.

Residential Segregation

There are many types of residential segregation, but it is racial segregation that currently poses the most difficult problems for education. It is helpful at the very start of a discussion of segregation to present an objective definition. If there were no racial residential segregation, white and Negro families would be similarly distributed among the housing of a city. Every residential neighborhood—a block or a cluster of blocks—would have about the same proportion of whites and Negroes as every other neighborhood. To the extent that there is a dissimilarity in the territorial distribution of white and Negro families, there is residential segregation. By this approach, segregation is simply observed fact. The processes by which the segregation came about may include prejudice, discrimination, income differences, choice and so forth, and there may be dispute about the relative importance of each of these causes. But the fact itself cannot reasonably be disputed.

The decennial censuses give the racial population of each city block. With these data I have calculated segregation indexes—measures of the dissimilarity in territorial distribution of whites and nonwhites—for all large cities in the United States. These indexes show that racial residential segregation is everywhere pronounced—in the North and in the South, in the recent past and in the present. This segregation by race is greater than the segregation of European immigrant groups ever was, and is much greater than the segregation of rich from poor of each race. The long-run trend in both North and South has been for racial residential segregation to increase. In the 1950s, this trend seems to have been (temporarily) halted in the North, as a result of the relatively loose housing market, rapid growth of urban Negro populations and increasing economic status of many Negro families. Speculation that the 1950s represented the beginnings of a general process of residential desegregation remains, so far, speculation. For a dozen or so cities which had special censuses in the mid-1960s, there is no indication of continued or accelerating declines in racial segregation since 1960. In many cities, an increasing supply of good housing is opening up to Negroes, and individual Negroes may be finding it easier to obtain housing in predominantly white neighborhoods. But the total picture continues to be one of very pronounced segregation, with no clear signs that fair housing legislation, educational campaigns, improved Negro economic status or any other factor has yet had a decisive impact.

These facts about residential segregation cannot, in my view, reasonably be disputed. There is more room for argument about the causes and prospects. With respect to causes, I am convinced that discrimination in the housing market is the principal cause, and that "choice" and "Negro poverty" are vastly overrated as contributing factors. Perhaps Negroes prefer to live in Negro neighborhoods, perhaps not. Consider the other side of the coin: the preference of whites for white neighborhoods. Such a preference, if it exists to any great extent, can hardly be considered apart from the prevalent prejudice and discrimination in our society. So long as any Negroes who move into white neighborhoods are threatened with physical violence or even simply social ostracism, it is hardly an expression of free choice for Negroes to prefer Negro neighborhoods.

The poverty argument is similarly easy to dispute. In the first place, Negro poverty itself is a result of prejudice and discrimination. But the real estate industry tends to argue that it cannot be responsible for that. All it can do is operate on the free market principle of selling to anyone who can afford the price. But it is patent nonsense to argue that the housing market in any large city in the country functions that way. Wealthy Negroes do not have the same housing options as wealthy whites. Poor Negroes do not live interspersed with poor whites.

This perspective on the causes of residential segregation does not permit any magic insights into the future. It is clear that a rapid increase in Negro incomes would not of itself lead to residential desegregation. Negroes of higher incomes are just as segregated as those of lower incomes. The impact of fair housing laws is difficult to foresee. Clearly, in the short run, there is likely to be little effect. Even federal regulations and laws seem to be enforced with the deliberate speed of the Supreme

Court school decision. Local ordinances already in existence in many states and cities have thus far failed to effect major changes in segregated residential patterns.

In the longer perspective, it is clear that the situation is changing, and changing rather rapidly compared to the pace of many deep-seated social revolutions. The degree of token integration has clearly increased; many neighborhoods have proved their tolerance by "allowing" a Negro family or two to live amongst them. The number of neighborhoods with a substantial degree of racial intermixture, stable over several years, is probably increasing. Once such patterns are shown to be not only possible, but profitable, not only utopian, but practical and just, will this innovation spread rapidly? Will the diffusion follow the accelerating curve of color television ownership or use of the birth control pill? Or will it diffuse more slowly, as seems to have been the case with religious and ethnic tolerance in general?

Whatever the answer, the short-run prospect is one of extreme racial residential segregation, and desegregation at a snail's pace (to the extent it occurs at all). Many cities already have a Negro majority in their public school systems. Many more cities will soon reach this point. The housing stock of central cities grows older. The white population, especially young families with children, continues to favor suburban over city residence, while similar Negro families continue to be confined to the cities. Private school systems augment th racial imbalance still further. The racial composition of city schools is becoming more homogeneously Negro. This occurs whether or not the pattern of segregated public schools changes, simply because the relative number of Negroes increases. As Negro children replace white children in a public school system, administrators, even if they attempt to utilize the available repertoire of desegregation techniques, are likely to find the number of Negroes in predominantly Negro schools increasing. In other words, the demographic composition of public school children is changing so rapidly that even if the all-white schools are integrated, the other schools will simultaneously become more predominantly Negro.

A recent Office of Education study demonstrated that Negro educational achievement, controlling for various relevant factors, is lower as the percentage of Negroes in a school increases. It argued further that most kinds of financial investment in schools had relatively little demonstrable payoff in terms of educational achievement. The United States Commission on Civil Rights drew from these findings a policy implication for the federal government to push for school desegregation nationwide. Compensatory educational schemes and additional investment in ghetto schools may be necessary stopgaps, the Commission argued, but they should not be allowed to divert money, time or energy from the desegregation move. The *New York Times,* among other editorial voices, countered that rapid school desegregation in our major metropolitan areas is a utopian dream. Children currently in school should not be shortchanged of urgently needed funds in the hopes of eventual salvation by federally imposed desegregation.

Educational administrators cannot embrace both positions wholeheartedly. The resources simply aren't available, and moves in one direction today may constrain future moves in another direction. It is clear that no decision can be made on educational grounds alone. Rather it is necessary to view the changing educational system in the context of a changing society. I have sketched a demographer's perspective on several aspects of our changing society—urbanization and suburbanization, migration, the movement of successive birth cohorts through the school system, and the awesome tenacity of racial residential segregation. The demography of education cannot be divorced from the general social demography of the nation. Similarly, I suggest, the resulting problems for the educational system should be viewed (by educators and by the public) neither as solely within the domain of the school systems nor as constraints to which we can only adapt. Study of population trends, especially migration and residential relocation, should be prominent on the nation's social policy agenda.

FURTHER READING:

Louise V. Kennedy, *The Negro Peasant Turns Cityward* (New York: Columbia University Press, 1930).

Karl E. Taeuber and Alma F. Taeuber, "The Changing Character of Negro Migration," *American Journal of Sociology*, (January, 1965).

E. G. Ravenstein, "The Laws of Migration," *Journal of the Royal Statistical Society*, (1885).

Karl E. Taeuber and Alma F. Taeuber, "White Migration and Socio-Economic Differences between Cities and Suburbs," *American Sociological Review*, (October, 1964).

U.S. Commission on Civil Rights, *Racial Isolation in the Public Schools*, Vol. 1 (Washington: U.S. Government Printing Office, 1967).

Karl E. Taeuber and Alma F. Taeuber, *Negroes in Cities* (Chicago: Aldine Publishing Co., 1965).

James S. Coleman *et al., Equality of Educational Opportunity* (Washington: U.S. Government Printing Office, 1966).

Of Achievement, Hope and Time in Poverty

JULES HENRY

Among the children of the very poor survival must take
precedence over every other consideration. But current
motivational theory tends to downgrade immediate and
physical motives. It turns its eagle vision instead, like a
rising young executive, on "goal-striving," "status-
seeking" and "planning." By such elite and middle-class
standards the poor must be said to have little or no
motivation.

Under a grant from the National Institute of Mental
Health we have been studying a large St. Louis housing
development inhabited almost exclusively by very poor
Negroes. We middle-class observers have noted the
pronounced tendency of the tenants toward "random-
like" and unrealistic behavior. Their attitudes toward
space, time, objects and persons lack our patterns of
organization, lack our predictability—even sometimes
seem to lack sense . . . to us. How do they seem to the

project dwellers themselves? After more than a year of field work with about 50 families we have the strong impression that they are well aware of the differences.

For instance, they make a strong distinction between C.P. (colored people's) time and W.P. (white people's) time. According to C.P. time a scheduled event may occur at any moment over a wide spread of hours—or perhaps not at all. They believe, however, that in the highly organized world of the whites it occurs when scheduled.

The housing project is so isolated from the social and economic life of the city and the white community that the occupational classes of the census bureau scarcely apply to it. The tenants work as domestics, or in the nooks and cracks of our economy; employment is uncertain, pay is poor, resources are scarce. Yet unemployed men talk of jobs they do not have, and the women in this "city of women" speak of husbands dead, fled or who never existed.

Illusion is thus a way of life. Young and old spend money they do not have for expensive clothes and cars. People with no power and status brag of influence and position and concentrate on getting the better of each other. The illusion of middle-class success settles invisibly over them. Thus a white school teacher working with Negro children remarks that they are not interested in solid accomplishment but only in showing off. Obviously such short-cutting must interfere with learning and with facing school and life realistically.

Casting out the poor and the Negro from white society has resulted in a social life so saturated by illusion that the fancy soon becomes the only possible achievement.

Disorganization and a life of dreams fit into the social

dynamic of the school room to create educational under-achievement.

The children of disorganization cannot create class-room organization; and the teacher can only work with those who have somehow managed to acquire enough of the necessary motivation. Often we have seen a harassed teacher working with a very few children in a class and trying to ignore the disorder and uproar the others are creating. Here are some notes made in one such sixth grade classroom, with both Negro and white children:

> The teacher was leaning over Paul's desk helping him with arithmetic. Irv and Mike were watching. Alice was talking to Jane and Joan to Edith. Nearby Alan, Ed and Tom were pushing and shoving. Tom got out of his seat, made a wad of notebook paper and tossed it into the air several times. Tom and Ed suddenly slammed their desks shut, got up and walked out noisily, Lila and Alice followed. Alan grinned at the observer, waved his hand, and said, "Hi." The teacher took no notice. . . .

This process of *partial withdrawal*—whereby the teacher simply withdrew to those few students she could handle—may occur anywhere an individual tries to cope with a disturbed environment; I have also seen it in mental hospitals. It reflects not so much the relationship between authority and client but the total social situation.

In school pupils have the choice of building status either with their teacher or their friends; to many, reputation among friends may be much more important. The pressure of peer-groups is very strong, and self-destructive status choice can occur in any such conflict between the demands of authority figures and the demands of the group. What usually tips the balance toward teacher and self-preservation is a measure of hope in the future. Disorganization can tip the balance the other way.

This is especially true if the disorganization has unique attractions for the children. In integrated classrooms, the approval of white students may become so attractive to Negro children that they gladly risk official displeasure, punishment or failure. In coeducational classes, attracting the attention and getting the approval of the opposite sex can become much more important than "teacher's dirty looks." All such "split" situations introduce disturbing and competing elements. Students can make status choices that ruin their whole future lives.

Very, very poor children, both by feeling and understanding, lack the structure on which conventional education can build. Their background does not have the elements of order necessary to achieve. Their homes are crowded, full of disturbance, physically and personally disorganized; they do not operate on schedules that pay much attention to school concepts of time. They lack both belief in achievement and fear of no achievement.

When 30 to 50 such children are in a class supposed to be run by one teacher, disorganization must result. From it the teacher in sheer self-defense may select only those elements suited to her task—she will teach those considered teachable and let the others go. But even the children most willing and able to learn are under tremendous pressure from their classmates to give up and join them. By pleasing the teacher they can buy success in a vague and distant future only at the probable expense of making their present life lonely, unhappy and even dangerous.

The poor motivation of the low-achiever is not therefore a demon somehow arising from and locked up inside himself but one effect of a whole sea of pressure and pain which has surrounded him since birth; and in which he himself seldom knows why he gasps.

But why all this disorder, illusion and destruction? Does it come about because, as some moralists believe, the poor lack an essential fiber, so that they tack and waver in the wind against which *we* advance?

This view is actually not far wrong. The poor do lack a fundamental vitamin that we others absorb with the smell of food, with the promise of gifts at Christmas, with plans for graduation. *They lack the essential strength of hope.*

Hope is not a simple nutrient. It goes straight to the heart of organization and makes it work.

Among lower animals organization occurs largely through in born genetic factors. With man, things are not so direct, and the word "culture" has been chosen to designate the complex learnings that determine his behavior.

But "culture" varies between societies and even between groups within societies. For the middle and upper classes in our society, achievement and security are major determinants. They organize behavior—or our behavior is organized around them. They act as carrots; the fear of their opposites—failure and insecurity—acts as a goad. When people do not see success and failure as we do, their behavior will appear to us random and purposeless; and we disapprove of it. But those who cannot hope for achievement or security can have no concept of the organization of behavior through time towards goals.

The culture of the middle class itself has been superficially charted. How, for instance, does the middle class handle hope, time and the self? Achievement depends on hope—and hope rests on time. Some time in the future we hope to achieve something. Even to say "Billy has stopped wetting the bed" means that desired change has occurred through time: Billy used to wet the bed but does so no longer.

But the parent with no hope can have only partial understanding of his child's having stopped bed-wetting. He can have no fruitful conception of the conscious movement through time toward desired goals. Relative to large social goals, his actions are undirected.

Though the poor have little hope for life, they do not wish to die. According to comparative suicide rates they have less taste for final voluntary quietus than any other class. Therefore, they concentrate on those factors that keep them alive—now—that make direct, obvious and strong contributions to present life. The culture of the very poor is a *flight from death*.

In this setting, the very disregard of common methods of looking at things and objects—such as how to arrange a house—can become institutionalized, a way of life. Such disregard in objects we call disorder; in behavior we call it randomness.

Martin Heidegger in *Being and Time* relates perception of self to existence through time. When people think of themselves they seem to say, he argues, "That is the way I was, this is how I am now, and in the future, I hope to be something else." These perceptions of self have past, present and future; and it is from them, he believes, that we conceive time. They presuppose change during time—movement from what used to be toward what will be. Self must therefore exist at least partly as a function of time; it must include organization through time.

But what happens to a person who has no expectations or hopes for himself or his children? His behavior, having neither background nor direction, is disorganized. What is left of him in the irreducible ash—the survival self—the flight from death.

The survival self has no real sublimation or higher displacement—nothing but physical life—in a very limited but very intense form. The survival self must concentrate on those experiences which give it continual and vivid reassurance that it is alive—heightened perhaps and smoothed by drugs or alcohol. It must, literally, keep *feeling* its life. Sociologists of middle-class background contemptuously refer to this state as "hedonism"—living for pleasure. It is not—it is flight from death.

The famous second law of thermodynamics states, in paraphrase, that disorder within an isolated system can only increase. Life is not pure physics; but there is a useful parallel. Consider a middle-class neighborhood or suburb. It is not an isolated system. Its members go out into the community, and the community comes in at the door and the mind. The resources of the community are known to and used by it, and it is subject to steady cultural and economic stimulation—which it in turn affects. The interaction brings adjustment and regulation; the disorder or randomness—"entropy" in the language of physics—is low.

The slum or lower-class housing project does not have access to these sources of support and stimulation. A paradox—or vicious circle—exists: because of their disorganization and lack of hope the very poor cannot or do not get to the major sources of economic and cultural stimulation; and their disorganization and hopelessness came in the first place from lack of access to these resources. Cut off from hope, stimulation and change, the poor neighborhood is an isolated human thermodynamic system, and its disorganization can only increase.

Many middle-class selves are also in flight from death; but they are trained to look at life through the lens of achievement, sustained by hope and expectation, and they can fly along this path—perhaps even to greater achievement. This sustenance is not available to the great majority from the slum and housing project.

Our conclusion then must be that hope is a boundary: it separates the free from the slave, the determined from the drifting—and the very poorest from almost all those above it. A corollary conclusion—even more surprising—follows: time, space and objects really exist for us only when we have hope.

Short of reforming his world, how can we stimulate the slum child to greater school achievement? Certainly it will not be enough to merely improve teaching methods and curricula. We must improve the school as a social system.

Some proposals are in order:

☐ *Building up perceptions.* Children whose central milieu involves so much disorganization and disorder cannot master mathematics, or any other discipline involving order and direction. I would urge that these children be given pre-school training in which the basic perceptions that other children acquire without apparent effort be deliberately taught. For instance, a child must learn fundamental shapes and categories—

insideness and outsideness, roundness, straightness, flexibility, rigidity, transparency, opacity, motion in a straight line, motion in a circle, rocking motion and many other basic perceptions. A child should have this perceptual competence before he starts school.

□ *Calming down.* Poor children often come to school unfed, after wretched nights torn by screaming, fighting, bed-wetting; often they cannot sleep because of cold and rats. They come to class hungry, sleepy and emotionally upset. To start routine schoolwork effectively at once is impossible. I propose that teachers be specially trained—as they are in the Youth Development Project of the greater Kansas City Mental Health Foundation—to deal with such children, and that they eat breakfast with them in school. The school should, of course, furnish the food, perhaps out of government surplus. School breakfast would accomplish two things: it would feed hungry children, otherwise unable to concentrate adequately on their work; and it would bring teacher and pupil together in an informal and friendly atmosphere, associated with satisfaction, before the strain of classroom constriction and peer-group pressures dictate that teacher become an enemy. It is essential, therefore, that the teacher be present. A program like this suggested by me in Kansas City brought about immediate and sharp improvement in attendance, behavior and in schoolwork. The more the teachers know about the emotional management of these children, the better.

□ *Expansion of participation.* The frequently proclaimed immediate goal of instruction—more personalized attention—is especially important with low-achievers. This can be done by reducing class size or by increasing the number of teachers. The extra teachers, if not as highly qualified as the regulars, should neverthe-less be trained and familiar with the lessons. They can be substitutes, teachers in training or even members of the domestic counterpart of the Peace Corps whenever that is established. They should be able to help with routine tasks, with keeping order—and with seeing to it that each child has more time, attention, care and opportunity to learn.

Very poor children need hope in order to achieve. So do those who work with them.

March/April 1965

How Teachers Learn
to Help Children Fail

ESTELLE FUCHS

Ideally, public schools exist to educate the child. But a high percentage of pupils fail as early as the fifth or sixth grade, especially in the urban slums. For many children, the educational process bogs down at a time when it has barely begun. Now, educators and social scientists have proposed a number of theories to explain this high rate of failure among slum-school children. One of them is that the slum-school system's tacit belief that social conditions outside the school make such failures inevitable *does* make such failures inevitable.

How this expectation of failure affects the instruction of lower-class children and becomes a self-fulfilling prophecy is suggested in data collected by Hunter College's Project TRUE (Teacher Resources for Urban Education), a study that focused on the experiences of 14 fledgling teachers in New York's inner-city elementary schools. As part of the study, several new teachers tape-recorded accounts of their first-semester teaching experiences in "special service" schools— schools that invariably had high Negro or Puerto Rican enrollments, retarded reading levels among the students, and constant discipline problems.

The following excerpts from one teacher's account show how the slum school gradually instills, in even the best-intentioned teacher, the prevailing rationale for its own failure: the idea that in the slum, it is the child and the family who fail, but never the school.

October 26

Mrs. Jones, the sixth-grade teacher, and I were discussing reading problems. I said, "I wonder about my children. They don't seem too slow; they seem average. Some of them even seem to be above average. I can't understand how they can grow up to be fifth- and sixth-graders and still be reading on the second-grade level. It seems absolutely amazing."

Mrs. Jones [an experienced teacher] explained about the environmental problems that these children have. "Some of them never see a newspaper. Some of them have never been on the subway. The parents are so busy having parties and things that they have no time for their children. They can't even take them to a museum or anything. It's very important that the teacher stress books."

Mrs. Jones tells her class, "If anyone asks you what you want for Christmas, you can say you want a book." She told me that she had a 6-1 class last year, and it was absolutely amazing how many children had never even seen a newspaper. They can't read Spanish either. So she said that the educational problem lies with the parents. They are the ones that have to be educated.

It's just a shame that the children suffer. This problem will take an awful lot to straighten it out. I guess it won't take one day or even a year; it will take time.

December 14

Here I am, a first-grade teacher. I get a great thrill out of these children being able to read but I often wonder, "Am I teaching them how to read or are they just stringing along sight words that they know?" I never had a course in college for teaching phonetics to children. In this school we have had conferences about it, but I really wish that one of the reading teachers would come in and specifically show me how to go about teaching phonetics. I have never gotten a course like this and it is a difficult thing, especially when there is a language barrier and words are quite strange to these children who can't speak English. How can they read English? We have a great responsibility on our shoulders and teachers should take these things seriously.

January 4

Something very, very important and different has happened to me in my school. It all happened the last week before the vacation on Tuesday. Mr. Frost, our principal, came over to me and asked if I would be willing to take over a second-grade class starting after the vacation. Well, I looked at him and I said, "Why?"

He told me briefly that the registers in the school have dropped and according to the board of education the school must lose a teacher. Apparently he was getting rid of a second-grade teacher and he wanted to combine two of the first-grade classes. The registers on the first grade were the lowest in the school, I believe. Anyway, he told me that he was going to all the afternoon first-grade teachers asking if any of them would be willing to change in the middle of the term. He said he thought perhaps someone would really want it and, instead of his just delegating a person, it would be better if he asked each one individually.

I was torn between many factors. I enjoyed my class very, very much and I enjoyed teaching the first grade. But because I was teaching afternoon session (our school runs on two different sessions), I was left out of many of the goings-on within the school as my hours were different and it also sort of conflicted with my home responsibilities. Well, with these two points in mind, I really felt that I would rather stay with my class than to switch over in the middle of the term.

But he explained further that some of the classes would not remain the same because there would be many changes made. So, being the type of person that I am, I felt that, even though I did want to stay with my class and the children and the first grade, if something had to be done in the school, there was no way of stopping it and I might as well do it. I explained to Mr. Frost that even though I wouldn't want to change in the middle—after all it would be a whole new experience, two classes of children would be suffering by the change—but if it had to be done I would be willing to take on the new responsibility.

With that, Mr. Frost said, "Thank you," and said he would go around to the other teachers to see if anyone really wanted to change. Well, already I felt that it was going to be me, but I wasn't sure.

A little later on in the day I was taking my class to recess, and we were lining up in the hall. I spoke to Miss Lane, another teacher, and she said that he had also spoken to her. At that point Mr. Frost came over and told me that he was sorry but that I had been the one elected. Well, I said that I hoped that I would be able to do a good job, and that was that.

From that point on, there was an awful lot of talk in the school. Everybody was talking about it, at least, everyone who knew something about the matter. So all the afternoon first-grade teachers and all the morning first-grade teachers knew, and many of the new teachers (those that I came into the school with), and apparently there was a lot of business going on that I can't begin to describe because I don't know how the whole thing started in the first place. However, from the office I did find out that it wasn't Mr. Frost's fault or anything that the second-grade teacher was going to be dismissed. It was a directive from higher up that stated he would lose a teacher. How he chose this particular teacher to let go I really can't say. I understand that they really didn't get along too well and neither of them were too happy in the school working together.

Everything went so quickly and everybody was talking to me. Mrs. Parsons spoke to me. She is my assistant principal. She was supervisor of the first grade and she will be in charge of the second grade also. I was told that I would have to take over the new class on January 2, the first day that we return from the vacation. I really felt terrible about my children, but it was something that had to be done and I did it.

Thursday, Mr. Frost talked to the other afternoon teachers and myself. He referred to me as the hero and he said, "Now it's your turn to be heroes also." He asked the afternoon first-grade teachers if they would be willing to have their registers become higher by having my 27 children split up among the four remaining afternoon classes, or did they think he should have them split up among all the first-grade classes, some of which met in the morning.

He was straightforward, saying that he didn't think it would be a good idea for the children to be split up among all the first-grade teachers. I agreed with him. He felt that it would be trying on the parents and on the children to have a whole new schedule worked out. After all, if you're used to going to school from 12 to 4, coming to school from 7:30 to 12 is quite a difference. It would be very, very hard on the parents. Especially in this neighborhood where sometimes they have a few children in the same grade, a few in different grades. So I agreed with Mr. Frost. The other teachers didn't seem too happy about the idea, but they said they would go along with it.

Mr. Frost and Mrs. Parsons worked out a plan whereby the 1-1 class register would go up to 35 which is generally what a 1-1 class has. The 1-3 class register would go up to 32 or 33. And so forth down the line. 1-5 (my class) would be erased. The teachers didn't think it was so bad then, but we all did have added responsibilities.

Mr. Frost then added that if we had any children in our classes that we felt did not belong, this was our chance to have them changed, since there would be many interclass transfers in order to make more homogeneous classes. So we all had to sit down and think—"Who belongs? Who doesn't belong?" I, of course, had to decide where 27 children would belong.

I went through my class and divided them into groups to the best of my ability. In the 1-1 class, I put Joseph R., who scored the highest on the reading-readiness test. As a result of his score and his work in class, I felt Joseph did belong in the 1-1 class. Lydia A., who I believe is a very smart girl and who wasn't really working as well as she could in my class, I felt belonged in the 1-1 class. Lydia scored second highest on the reading-readiness test. In the 1-1 class, I also put Anita R. Anita is a bit older than the rest of the children but she has caught on most beautifully to most phases of school work even though she just came to the United States last March. Also, she scored the same as Lydia on the reading-readiness test.

Then I decided that I would put Robert M. in the 1-1 class. I felt strongly that Robert was by far the best child in my class. Robert did every bit of the work ever assigned. He caught on very, very quickly to all phases of work besides doing his work well, quickly, efficiently and neatly. Even though on reading-readiness he only scored in the 50th percentile, I felt he really stood out and I also felt that once you're in a "1" class, unless you really don't belong, you have a better chance. The "1" class is really the only class that you would term a "good" class. So those four children I recommended for the 1-1 class.

Then I went down the line and for the 1-3 class, I picked nine children, really good children who, on the whole, listened and did their work. Most of them scored in the 50th and 40th percentile on reading-readiness, and they were coping with school problems very, very well. In the 1-7 class, I put the slower children and in the 1-9 class, of course, which is Mrs. Gould's, I put all the children that really weren't doing well in school work at all. First, Alberto S. Alberto who is still not able to write his name. Then I put Beatrice L., Stella S., Pedro D., and several others, who really were not working well, in the 1-9 class.

I know that the other teachers do have a big job

before them because whichever class these children are placed in will not have been doing exactly the same work. The children either have much to catch up on or they might review some of the work, and the teachers will have to be patient either way. I really don't think anyone will have serious discipline problems, except perhaps in the 1-1 class where Lydia and Anita have been placed.

The time came when I had to tell the children that I would not be their teacher anymore. Well, as young as they are, I think that many of them caught on immediately, and before I could say anything, faces were very, very long and the children were mumbling, "But I wanted you for a teacher."

That was all I needed! I felt even worse than I felt when I found out that I wouldn't be with them anymore. So I continued talking and I told them that it's just something that happens and that I would still be in the school and maybe next year they would get me when they go to the second grade. I told them that I would miss them all, that they would have a lot of fun in their new classes, and they would learn a lot. And, of course, I said, "You know all the other teachers. Some of you will get Mrs. Lewis. Some will get Miss Lane, some will get Miss Taylor, and some will get Mrs. Gould.

To my astonishment Anita kept saying over and over, "But I want you for a teacher. But I want you for a teacher."

I looked around the room. Most of the children were sitting there with very, very long faces. Joseph C. was sitting there with the longest face you could imagine, Robert G. said he didn't want another teacher, and all of a sudden Joseph started crying and just didn't stop. He cried all the way out into the hall when we got dressed to go home. I spoke to him softly and said, "Joseph, wouldn't you like Miss Lane for a teacher?" She was standing right near me, and finally he stopped crying.

I said goodbye to them and that I would see them all. And that was the end of my class . . . .

Good schools. Poor schools. What is a good school? Is a good school one that is in a good neighborhood, that has middle-class children? Is a poor school one in a depressed area where you have Negro and Puerto Rican children? These are common terms that people refer to all the time. They hear your school is on Wolf Street—"Oh, you must be in a bad school."

I don't really think that that is what a good or a bad school is. I think a good school is a school that is well run, has a good administration, has people that work together well, has good discipline and where the children are able to learn and also, of course, where there are numerous facilities for the children and the teachers. In my estimation a poor or a bad school would be one in which the administration and the teachers do not work together, are not working in the best interests of the children and where learning is not going on. Also, a poor school is one where you don't have proper facilities. I am not acquainted with many of the public schools, and I really can't say that the ones that I know are better or worse.

I believe my school is a pretty good school. It isn't in the best neighborhood. There are many, many problems in my school but on the whole I think that the teachers and the administration work together and I do believe that they are doing the best they can with the problems that are around.

You have to remember that in a school such as ours

the children are not as ready and willing to learn as in schools in middle-class neighborhoods.

When a new teacher enters the classroom, she must learn the behavior, attitudes and skills required in the new situation. Much of this learning is conscious. Some of it is not. What is significant is that, while on the job, the teacher is socialized to her new role—she is integrated into the society of the school, and learns the values, beliefs, and attitudes that govern its functioning.

The saga of class 1-5 shows the subtle ways in which one new teacher is socialized to her job. In just a few months, she accepts the demands of the school organization and its prevailing rationale for student failure.

The new teacher of class 1-5 in a slum school begins her career with a warm, friendly attitude toward her students. She respects and admires their abilities and is troubled by what the future holds for them: by the sixth grade in her school, educational failure is very common.

Very early in her teaching career, however, a more experienced teacher exposes this new teacher to the belief, widely held, that the children come from inferior backgrounds and that the deficits in their homes—expressed here as lack of newspapers and parental care—prevent educational achievement. That the teachers and the school as an institution contribute to the failure of the children is never even considered as a possible cause. The beginning teacher, in her description of what happens to class 1-5, then provides us with a graphic account of the ways in which this attitude can promote failure.

First, let us examine the actual instruction of the children. Early in her career, this new, very sincere teacher is painfully aware of her own deficiencies. Unsure about her teaching of so fundamental a subject as reading, she raises serious questions about her own effectiveness. As yet, she has not unconsciously accepted the notion that the failure of children stems from gaps in their backgrounds. Although no consensus exists about reading methodology, the teacher tells us that there are serious weaknesses in feedback evaluation—and that she is unable to find out what the children have been taught or what they have really learned.

By the end of the term, all this has changed. By that time, the eventual failure of most of class 1-5 has been virtually assured. And the teacher has come to rationalize this failure in terms of pupil inadequacy.

In the particular case of class 1-5, the cycle of failure begins with a drop in the number of students registered in the school. The principal loses a teacher, which in turn means dissolving a class and subsequently distributing its children among other classes. The principal and the teachers have no control over this event. In the inner-city schools, education budgets, tables of organization, and directions from headquarters create conditions beyond the control of the administrators and teachers who are in closest touch with the children.

A drop in pupil registers would seemingly provide the opportunity for a higher adult-pupil ratio and, consequently, more individualized instruction and pedagogical supports for both youngsters and teachers. In a suburban school, this is probably what would have occurred. But in this slum school, the register drop leads to the loss of a teacher, larger classes, and—perhaps most important—increased time spent by the administrator and his staff on the mechanics of administration rather than on the supervision of instruction. (Why *this* particular teacher is released is unclear, though her substitute status and low rank in the staff hierarchy probably contribute to her release.) As a result many classes are disrupted, several first-grade class registers grow larger, time for instruction is lost, and concern is felt by teachers and pupils alike.

An even more significant clue to the possible eventual failure of the children is described in poignant detail— when the teacher tells how the youngsters in her class are to be distributed among the other first-grade classes. Educators now know that children mature at different rates; that they have different rates of learning readiness; and that developmental differences between boys and girls are relevant to learning. To forecast the educational outcome of youngsters at this early state of their development, without due provision for these normal growth variations, is a travesty of the educational process. Yet here, in the first half of the first grade, a relatively inexperienced young teacher, herself keenly aware of her own deficiencies as an educator, is placed in the position of literally deciding the educational future of her charges.

A few are selected for success—"I felt that once you're in a '1' class, unless you really don't belong, you have a better chance. The '1' class is really the only class that you would term a 'good' class." Several children are placed in a class labeled "slow." And the remaining youngsters are relegated to a state of limbo, a middle range that does not carry the hope of providing a "better chance."

Thus, before these youngsters have completed a full four months of schooling, their educational futures have been "tracked": all through the grades, the labels of their class placement will follow them, accompanied by teacher attitudes about their abilities. Some youngsters are selected very early for success, others written off as slow. Because differential teaching occurs and helps to widen the gap between children, the opportunity to move from one category to another is limited. In addition, the children too become aware of the labels placed upon them. And their pattern for achievement in later years is influenced by their feelings of success or failure in early school experiences.

The teacher, as she reflects upon what a "good" or a "bad" school is, continues to include how well the children learn as a significant criterion, together with good relations between staff and administration. But the children in her school do not achieve very well academically, so when describing her school as "good," she stresses the good relations between the administration and the teachers. The fact that the children do not learn does not seem so important now: "the children are not as ready and willing to learn as in schools in middle-class neighborhoods."

How well our teacher has internalized the attitude that deficits of the children themselves explain their failure in school! How normal she now considers the administrative upheavals and their effects upon teachers and children! How perfectly ordinary she considers the "tracking" of youngsters so early in their school years!

The teacher of class 1-5 has been socialized by the school to accept its structure and values. Despite her sincerity and warmth and obvious concern for the children, this teacher is not likely to change the forecast of failure for most of these children—because she has come to accept the very structural and attitudinal factors that make failure nearly certain. In addition, with all her good intentions, she has come to operate as an agent determining the life chances of the children in her class—by distributing them among the ranked classes in the grade.

This teacher came to her job with very positive impulses. She thought highly of her youngsters and was disturbed that, with what appeared to be good potential, there was so much failure in the school in the upper grades. She looked inward for ways in which she might improve her efforts to forestall retardation. She was not repelled by the neighborhood in which she worked. There is every indication that she had the potential to become a very effective teacher of disadvantaged youngsters.

Her good impulses, however, were not enough. This young teacher, unarmed with the strength that understanding the social processes involved might have given her and having little power within the school hierarchy, was socialized by the attitudes of those around her, by the administration, and by the availability of a suitable rationale to explain her and the school's failure to fulfill their ideal roles. As a result she came to accept traditional slum-school attitudes toward the children—and traditional attitudes toward school organization as the way things have to be. This teacher is a pleasant, flexible, cooperative young woman to have on one's staff. But she has learned to behave and think in a way that perpetuates a process by which disadvantaged children continue to be disadvantaged.

The organizational structure of the large inner-city school and the attitudes of the administrators and teachers within it clearly affect the development of the children attending. No theory proposed to explain the academic failure of poor and minority-group children

can ignore the impact of the actual school experience
and the context in which it occurs.

September 1968

The Self-Fulfilling Prophecy in Ghetto Education

RAY C. RIST

Teacher-student relationships and the dynamics of interaction between teacher and students are far from uniform. For any child within the classroom, variations in the experience of success or failure, praise or ridicule, freedom or control, creativity or docility, comprehension or mystification may ultimately have significance far beyond the classroom. This chapter will explore what is generally regarded as a crucial aspect of the classroom experience for the children involved—the process whereby expectations and social interactions give rise to the social organization of the class. During this process, out of a large group of children and an adult unknown to one another prior to the beginning of the school year, emerges patterns of behavior, expectations of performance, and a mutually accepted stratification system delineating those doing well from those doing poorly.

A number of studies have sought to determine what effect on children a teacher's values, beliefs, attitudes and expectations may have. Many researchers have noted that how a teacher expects a pupil to perform may have a strong influence on his actual academic performance. They have sought to validate a type of educational self-fulfilling prophecy: if the teacher expects high performance she receives it, and vice versa. But few if any of these studies have explained either the basis upon which such differential expectations are formed or how they are manifested within the classroom. Here we shall attempt to answer these questions, by describing both the factors that are critical in the teacher's development of expectations for various groups of her pupils and the process by which such expectations influence the classroom experience.

Data for this study were collected by means of twice weekly one and one-half hour observations of a single group of black children in an urban ghetto school who began kindergarten in September of 1967. Formal observations were conducted throughout the year while the children were in kindergarten and again in 1969 when these same children were in the first half of their second-grade year. The children were also visited informally four times in the classroom during their first-grade year. The difference between the formal and informal observations consisted in the fact that during formal visits, a continuous handwritten account was taken of classroom interaction and activity as it occurred. The informal observations did not include the taking of notes during the classroom visit, but comments were written after the visit. Additionally, a series of interviews were conducted with both the kindergarten and the second-grade teachers. No mechanical devices were utilized to record classroom activities or interviews.

The particular school which the children attend was built in the early part of the 1960s. It has classes from kindergarten through the eighth grade and a single special education class. The enrollment fluctuates near the 900 level while the teaching staff consists of 26 teachers, in addition to a librarian, two physical education instructors, the principal and an assistant principal. There are also at the school, on a part time basis, a speech therapist, social worker, nurse and doctor, all employed by the Board of Education. All administrators, teachers, staff and pupils are black. (The author is Caucasian.) The school is located in a blighted urban area that has 98 percent black population within its census district. Within the school itself, nearly 500 of the 900 pupils (55 percent) come from families supported by funds from Aid to Dependent Children. I do not believe that this school and the classrooms within it are atypical from others in urban black neighborhoods.

The school in which this study occurred was selected by the District Superintendent as one of five available to the research team. All five schools were visited during the course of the study and detailed observations were conducted in four of them. The principal at the school reported upon in this study commented that I was very fortunate in coming to his school since his staff (and kindergarten teacher in particular) were equal to "any in the city."

The Kindergarten Class

Prior to the beginning of the school year, the teacher possessed several different kinds of information regarding the children that she would have in her class. The first was the preregistration form, which gave the name of the child, his age, the name of his parents, his home address, his phone number and whether he had had any preschool experience. The second source of information was a tentative list of all children enrolled in the kindergarten class who lived in homes that received public welfare funds, and was provided by the school social worker.

Third, an interview was held with the mother and child during the registration period in the few days prior to the beginning of school or during the first days of school. Medical information and any specific paternal concern related to the child were gathered. This latter information was noted on the "Behavioral Question- naire" where the mother was to indicate her concern, if any, on 28 different items. Such items as thumb- sucking, bed-wetting, loss of bowel control, lying, stealing, fighting and laziness were included on this questionnaire.

The fourth source of information was the teachers' experiences with older siblings. A rather strong informal norm had developed among teachers in the school such that pertinent information, especially that related to discipline matters, was passed on to the next teacher of the student. Frequently, during the first days of the school year, there were admonitions to a specific teacher to "watch out" for a child believed to be a "troublemaker." Teachers would also relate techniques of controlling the behavior of a student who had been disruptive in the class. Thus a variety of information concerning students in the school was shared, whether that information regarded academic performance, be- havior in class or the parents and their interest in the student and the school.

When the kindergarten teacher made the permanent seating assignments on the eighth day of school, not only had she the above four sources of information concerning the children, but she had also had time to observe them within the classroom setting. Thus the behavior, degree and type of verbalization, dress, mannerisms, physical appearance and performance on the early tasks assigned during class were available to her as she began to form opinions concerning the capabilities and potential of the various children. There seems to be little doubt that such evaluation of the children by the teacher was beginning. Within a few days, only a certain group of children were continually being called on to lead the class in the Pledge of Allegiance, read the weather calendar each day, come to the front for "show and tell" periods, take messages to the office, count the number of children present in the class, pass out materials for class projects, be in charge of equipment on the playground, and lead the class to the bathroom, library or on a school tour. This one group of children, that continually were physically close to the teacher and had a high degree of verbal interaction with her, she placed at Table 1.

As one progressed from Table 1 to Table 2 and Table 3, there was an increasing dissimilarity between each group of children at the different tables on at least four major criteria. The first criterion appeared to be the physical appearance of the child. While the children at Table 1 were all dressed in clean clothes that were relatively new and pressed, most of the children at Table 2, and with only one exception at Table 3, were all quite poorly dressed. The clothes were old and often quite dirty. The children at Tables 2 and 3 also had a noticeably different quality and quantity of clothes to wear, especially during the winter months. Whereas the children at Table 1 would come on cold days with heavy coats and sweaters, the children at the other two tables often wore very thin spring coats and summer clothes. The single child at Table 3 who came to school quite nicely dressed came from a home in which the mother was receiving welfare funds, but was supplied with clothing for the children by the families of her brother and sister.

An additional aspect of the physical appearance of the children related to their body odor. While none of the children at Table 1 came to class with an odor of urine on them, there were two children at Table 2 and five children at Table 3 who frequently had such an odor. There was not a clear distinction among the children at the various tables as the the degree of "blackness" of their skin, but there were more children at the third table with very dark skin (five in all) than there were at the first table (three). There was also a noticeable distinction among the various groups of children as to the condition of their hair. While the three boys at Table 1 all had short hair cuts and the six girls at the same table had their hair "processed" and combed, the number of children with either matted or unprocessed hair increased at Table 2 (two boys and three girls) and eight of the children at Table 3 (four boys and four girls). None of the children in the kindergarten class wore their hair in the style of a "natural."

A second major criteria which appeared to differenti-ate the children at the various tables was their inter-action, both among themselves and with the teacher. The several children who began to develop as leaders within the class by giving directions to other members, initiating the division of the class into teams on the playground, and seeking to speak for the class to the teacher ("We want to color now"), all were placed by the teacher at Table 1. This same group of children displayed considerable ease in their interaction with her. Whereas the children at Tables 2 and 3 would often linger on the periphery of groups surrounding the teacher, the children at Table 1 most often crowded close to her.

The use of language within the classroom appeared to be the third major differentiation among the children. While the children placed at the first table were quite verbal with the teacher, the children placed at the remaining two tables spoke much less frequently with her. The children placed at the first table also displayed a greater use of Standard American English within the classroom. Whereas the children placed at the last two tables most often responded to the teacher in black dialect, the children at the first table did so very infrequently. In other words, the children at the first table were much more adept at the use of "school language" than were those at the other tables. The teacher utilized Standard American English in the classroom and one group of children was able to respond in a like manner. The frequency of a "no response" to a question from the teacher was recorded at a ratio of nearly three to one for the children at the last two tables as opposed to Table 1. When questions were asked, the children who were placed at the first table most often gave a response.

The final apparent criterion by which the children at the first table were quite noticeably different from those at the other tables consisted of a series of social factors which were known to the teacher prior to her seating the children. Though it is not known to what degree she utilized this particular criterion when she assigned seats, it does contribute to developing a clear profile of the children at the various tables. Table 1 gives a summary of the distribution of the children at the three tables on a series of variables related to social and family conditions. Such variables may be considered to give indication of the relative status of the children within the room, based on the income, education and size of the family.

Believing, as I do, that the teacher did not randomly assign the children to the various tables, it is necessary to indicate the basis for the seating arrangement. I would contend that the teacher developed, utilizing some combination of the four criteria outlined above, a series of expectations about the potential performance of each child and then grouped the children according to perceived similarities in expected performance. The teacher herself informed me that the first table consisted of her "fast learners" while those at the last two tables "had no idea of what was going on in the classroom." What becomes crucial in this discussion is to ascertain the basis upon which the teacher developed her criteria of "fast learner" since there had been no formal testing of the children as to their academic potential or capacity for cognitive development. She made evaluative judgements of their expected capacities to perform academic tasks after eight days of school.

Certain criteria became indicative of expected success and others became indicative of expected failure. Those children who closely fit the teacher's "ideal type" of the successful child were chosen for seats at Table 1. Those children that had the least "goodness of fit" with her ideal type were placed at the third table. The criteria

TABLE 1: Distribution of Socioeconomic Status Factors by Seating Arrangement at the Three Tables in the Kindergarten Classroom.

Factors	Seating Arrangement*		
	Table 1	Table 2	Table 3
Income			
1) Families on welfare	0	2	4
2) Families with father employed	6	3	2
3) Families with mother employed	5	5	5
4) Families with both parents employed	5	3	2
5) Total family income below $3,000./yr.**	0	4	7
6) Total family income above $12,000./yr.**	4	0	0
Education			
1) Father ever grade school	6	3	2
2) Father ever high school	5	2	1
3) Father ever college	1	0	0
4) Mother ever grade school	9	10	8
5) Mother ever high school	7	6	5
6) Mother ever college	4	0	0
7) Children with pre-school experience	1	1	0
Family Size			
1) Families with one child	3	1	0
2) Families with six or more children	2	6	7
3) Average number of siblings in family	3-4	5-6	6-7
4) Families with both parents present	6	3	2

*There are nine children at Table 1, eleven at Table 2, and ten children at Table 3.
**Estimated from stated occupation.

upon which a teacher would construct her ideal type of the successful student would rest in her perception of certain attributes in the child that she believed would make for success. To understand what the teacher considered as "success," one would have to examine her perception of the larger society and whom in that larger society she perceived as successful. I believe that the reference group utilized by Mrs. Caplow to determine what constituted success was a mixed black-white, well-educated middle class. (The names of all staff and students are pseudonyms.) Those attributes most desired by educated members of the middle class became the basis for her evaluation of the children. Highly prized middle-class status for the child in the classroom was attained by demonstrating ease of interaction among adults; high degree of verbalization in Standard American English; the ability to become a leader; a neat and clean appearance; coming from a family that is educated, employed, living together and interested in the child; and the ability to participate well as a member of a group.

The kindergarten teacher appeared to have been raised in a home where the above values were emphasized as important. Her mother was a college graduate, as were her brother and sisters. The family lived in the same neighborhood for many years, and the father held a responsible position with a public utility company in the city. The family was devoutly religious and those of the family still in the city attend the same church. She and other members of her family were active in a number of civil rights organizations in the city. The attributes indicative of "success" among those of the educated middle class had been attained by the teacher. She was a college graduate, held positions of respect and responsibility in the black community, lived in a comfortable middle-class section of the city in a well-furnished and spacious home, together with her husband earned over $20,000 per year, was active in a number of community organizations, and had parents, brother and sisters similar in education, income and occupational positions.

The teacher's preferential treatment of a select group of children appeared to be derived from her belief that certain behavioral and cultural characteristics are more crucial to learning in school than are others. In a similar manner, those children who appeared not to possess the criteria essential for success were ascribed low status and described as "failures" by the teacher. They were relegated to positions at Table 2 and 3. The placement of the children then appeared to result from their possessing or lacking the certain desired cultural characteristics perceived as important by the teacher.

The organization of the kindergarten classroom became the basis for the differential treatment of the children for the remainder of the school year. From the day that the class was assigned permanent seats, the activities in the classroom perceivably changed. The fundamental division of the class into those expected to learn and those expected not to permeated the teacher's orientation to the class.

The teacher's rationalization for narrowing her attention to selected students was that the majority of the remainder of the class (in her words) "just had no idea of what was going on in the classroom." Her reliance on the few students of ascribed high social status reached such proportions that on occasion, the teacher would use one of these students as an exemplar that the remainder of the class would do well to emulate.

(It is Fire Prevention Week and the teacher is trying to have the children say so. The children make a number of incorrect responses, a few of which follow:) Jim who had raised his hand, in answer to the question, "Do you know what week it is?" says, "October." The teacher says "No, that's the name of the month. Jane, do you know what special week this is?" and Jane responds, "It cold outside." Teacher says, "No, that is not it either. I guess I will have to call on Pamela. Pamela, come here and stand by me and tell the rest of the boys and girls what special week this is." Pamela leaves her chair, comes and stands by the teacher, turns and faces the rest of the class. The teacher puts her arm around Pamela, and Pamela says, "It fire week." The teacher responds, "Well Pamela, that is close, actually it is Fire Prevention Week."

On another occasion, the Friday after Hallowe'en, the teacher informed the class that she would allow time for all the students to come to the front of the class and tell of their experiences. She, in reality, called on six students, five of whom sat at Table 1 and the sixth at Table 2. Not only on this occasion, but on others, the teacher focused her attention on the experiences of the higher status students.

(The students are involved in acting out a skit arranged by the teacher on how a family should come together to eat the evening meal.) The students acting the roles of mother, father and daughter are all from Table 1. The boy playing the son is from Table 2. At the small dinner table set up in the center of the classroom, the four children are supposed to be sharing with each other what they had done during the day—the father at work, the mother at home and the two children at school. The Table 2 boy makes few comments. (In real life he has no father and his mother is supported by ADC funds.) The teacher comments, "I think that we are going to have to let Milt (Table 1) be the new son. Sam, why don't you go and sit down. Milt, you seem to be one who would know what a son is supposed to do at the dinner table. You come and take Sam's place."

In this instance, the lower-status student was penalized, not only for failing to have verbalized middle-class table talk, but more fundamentally for lacking middle-class experiences. He had no actual father to whom he could speak at the dinner table, yet he was expected to speak fluently with an imaginary one.

Though the blackboard was long enough to extend parallel to all three tables, the teacher wrote such assignments as arithmetic problems and drew all illustrations on the board in front of the students at Table 1. A rather poignant example of the penalty the children at Table 3 had to pay was that they often could not see the board material.

Lilly stands up out of her seat. Mrs. Caplow asks Lilly what she wants. Lilly makes no verbal response to the question. Mrs. Caplow then says rather firmly to Lilly, "Sit down." Lilly does. However, Lilly sits down sideways in the chair (so she is still facing the teacher). Mrs. Caplow instructs Lilly to put her feet under the table. This Lilly does. Now she is facing directly away from the teacher and the blackboard where the teacher is demonstrating to the students how to print the letter, "O."

The realization of the self-fulfilling prophecy within the classroom was in its final stages by late May of the kindergarten year. Lack of communication with the teacher, lack of involvement in the class activities and infrequent instruction all characterized the situation of the children at Tables 2 and 3. During one observational period of an hour in May, not a single act of communication was directed towards any child at either Table 2 or 3 by the teacher except for twice command- ing "sit down." The teacher devoted her attention to teaching those children at Table 1. Attempts by the children at Table 2 and 3 to elicit the attention of the teacher were much fewer than earlier in the school year.

In June, after school had ended for the year, the teacher was asked to comment on the children in her class. Of the children at the first table, she noted:

I guess the best way to describe it is that very few children in my class are exceptional. I guess you could notice this just from the way the children were seated this year. Those at Table 1 gave consistently the most responses throughout the year and seemed most interested and aware of what was going on in the classroom.

Of those children at the remaining two tables, the teacher commented:

It seems to me that some of the children at Table 2 and most all the children at Table 3 at times seem to have no idea of what is going on in the classroom and were off in another world all by themselves. It just appears that some can do it and some cannot. I don't think that it is the teaching that affects those that cannot do it, but some are just basically low achievers.

The students in the kindergarten classroom did not sit passively, internalizing the behavior the the teacher directed towards them. Rather, they responded to the stimuli of the teacher, both in internal differentiations within the class itself and also in their response to the teacher.

For the high-status students at Table 1, the response to the track system of the teacher appeared to be at least three-fold. One such response was the directing of ridicule and belittlement towards those children at Tables 2 and 3. At no point during the entire school year was a child from Table 2 or 3 ever observed directing such remarks at the children at Table 1.

Jim starts to say out loud that he is smarter than Tom. He repeats it over and over again, "I smarter than you. I smarter than you." (Jim sits at Table 1, Tom at Table 3.)

Milt came over to the observer and told him to look at Lilly's shoes. I asked him why I should and he replied, "Because they so ragged and dirty." (Milt is at Table 1, Lilly at Table 3.)

When I asked Lilly what it was that she was drawing, she replied, "A parachute." Gregory interrupted and said, "She can't draw nothin'."

The problems of those children who were of lower status were compounded, for not only had the teacher indicated her low esteem of them, but their peers had also turned against them. The implications for the future schooling of a child who lacks the desired status credentials in a classroom where the teacher places high value on middle-class "success" values and mannerisms are tragic.

It must not be assumed, however, that though the children at Tables 2 and 3 did not participate in classroom activities and were systematically ignored by the teacher, they did not learn. I contend that in fact they did learn, but in a fundamentally different way from the way in which the high-status children at Table

1 learned. The children at Table 2 and 3 who were
unable to interact with the teacher began to develop
patterns of interaction among themselves whereby they
would discuss the material that the teacher was presenting to the children at Table 1. Thus I have termed their
method of grasping the material "secondary learning" to
imply that knowledge was not gained in direct interaction with the teacher, but through the mediation of
peers and also through listening to the teacher though
she was not speaking to them. That the children were
grasping, in part, the material presented in the classroom, was indicated to me in home visits when the
children who sat at Table 3 would relate material
specifically taught by the teacher to the children at
Table 1. It is not that the children at Table 2 and 3 were
ignorant of what was being taught in the class, but
rather that the patterns of classroom interaction established by the teacher inhibited the low-status children
from verbalizing what knowledge they had accumulated.
From the teacher's terms of reference, those who could
not discuss must not know. Her expectations continued
to be fulfilled, for though the low-status children had
accumulated knowledge, they did not have the opportunity to verbalize it and, consequently, the teacher could
not know what they had learned.

A second response of the higher status students to the
differential behavior of the teacher towards them was to
seek solidarity and closeness with the teacher and urge
Table 2 and 3 children to comply with her wishes.

The teacher is out of the room. Pamela says to the
class, "We all should clean up before the teacher
comes." Shortly thereafter the teacher has still not
returned and Pamela begins to supervise other children in the class. She says to one girl from Table 3,

"Girl, leave that piano alone." The child plays only a short time longer and then leaves.

The teacher has instructed the students to go and take off their coats since they have come in from the playground. Milt says, "OK y'all, let's go take off our clothes."

When the teacher tells the students to come from their desks and form a semicircle around her, Gregory scoots up very close to Mrs. Caplow and is practically sitting in her lap.

Not only would the Table 1 students attempt to control and ridicule the Table 2 and 3 students, but they also perceived and verbalized that they, the Table 1 students, were better students and were receiving differential treatment from the teacher.

The children are rehearsing a play, Little Red Riding Hood. Pamela tells the observer, "The teacher gave me the best part." The teacher overheard this comment, smiled, and made no verbal response.

The children are preparing to go on a field trip to a local dairy. The teacher has designated Gregory as the "sheriff" for the trip. Mrs. Caplow stated that for the field trip today Gregory would be the sheriff. Mrs. Caplow simply watched as Gregory would walk up to a student and push him back into line saying, "Boy, stand where you suppose to." Several times he went up to students from Table 3 and showed them the badge that the teacher had given to him and said, "Teacher made me sheriff."

The children seated at the first table were internalizing the attitudes and behavior of the teacher towards those at the remaining two tables. That is, as the teacher responded from her reference group orientation as to which type of children were most likely to succeed and which type most likely to fail, she behaved towards the two groups of children in a significantly different manner. The children from Table 1 were also learning through emulating the teacher how to behave towards other black children who came from low-income and poorly educated homes. The teacher, who came from a well-educated and middle-income family, and the children from Table 1 who came from a background similiar to the teacher's, came to respond to the children from poor and uneducated homes in a strikingly similar manner.

The lower-status students in the classroom from Tables 2 and 3 responded in significantly different ways to the stimuli of the teacher. The two major responses of the Table 2 and 3 students were withdrawal and verbal and physical in-group hostility. The withdrawal took the form of physical withdrawal, but most often it was psychological.

Betty, a very poorly dressed child, had gone outside and hidden behind the door. . . . Mrs. Caplow sees Betty leave and goes outside to bring her back, says in an authoritative and irritated voice, "Betty, come here right now." When the child returns, Mrs. Caplow seizes her by the right arm, brings her over to the group and pushes her down to the floor. Betty begins to cry. . . . The teacher now shows the group a large posterboard with a picture of a white child going to school.

The teacher is demonstrating how to mount leaves between two pieces of wax paper. Betty leaves the group and goes back to her seat and begins to color. The teacher is instructing the children in how they can make a "spooky thing" for Hallowe'en. James turns away from the teacher and puts his head on his desk. Mrs. Caplow looks at James and says, "James, sit up and look here."

The teacher has the children seated on the floor in front of her asking them questions about a story that she had read to them. The teacher says, "June, your back is turned. I want to see your face." (The child had turned completely around and was facing away from the group.)

The verbal and physical hostility that the children at Tables 2 and 3 began to act out among themselves in many ways mirrored what the Table 1 students and the teacher were also saying about them. There are numerous instances in the observations of the children at Tables 2 and 3 calling one another "stupid," "dummy," or "dumb dumb." Racial overtones were noted on two occasions when one boy called another a "nigger," and on another occasion when a girl called a boy an "almond head." Threats of beatings, "whoppins," and even spitting on a child were also recorded among those at Tables 2 and 3. Also at Table 2, two instances were observed in which a single child hoarded all the supplies for the whole table. Similar manifestations of hostility were not observed among those children at the first table. A popular "folk myth" of American society is that children are inherently cruel to one another and that this tendency towards cruelty must be socialized into socially acceptable channels. The evidence from this classroom would indicate that much of the cruelty displayed was a result of the social organization of the class. Those children at Tables 2 and 3 who displayed cruelty appeared to have learned from the teacher that it was acceptable to act in an aggressive manner towards those from low-income and poorly educated backgrounds. Their cruelty was not diffuse, but rather focused on a specific group—the other poor children. Likewise, the incidence of such behavior increased over time. The children at Tables 2 and 3 did not begin the school year ridiculing and belittling each other. The children from the first table were also apparently socialized into a pattern of behavior in which they perceived that they could direct hostility and aggression towards those at Table 2 and 3, but not towards one another. The children in the class learned who was vulnerable to hostility and who was not through the actions of the teacher. She established the patterns of differential behavior which the class adopted.

First Grade

Though Mrs. Caplow had anticipated that only 12 of the children from the kindergarten class would attend the first grade in the same school, 18 of the children were assigned during the summer to the first-grade classroom in the main building. The remaining children either were assigned to a new school a few blocks north, or were assigned to a branch school designed to handle the overflow from the main building, or had moved away. Mrs. Logan, the first-grade teacher, had had more than 20 years of teaching experience in the city public school system, and every school in which she had taught was more than 90 percent black.

In the first-grade classroom, Mrs. Logan also divided the children into three groups. Those children whom she placed at "Table A" had all been Table 1 students in kindergarten. No student who had sat at Table 2 or 3 in kindergarten was placed at Table A in the first grade. Instead, all the students from Table 2 and 3—with one exception—were placed together at "Table B." At the third table, which Mrs. Logan called "Table C," she placed the nine children repeating the grade plus Betty who had sat at Table 3 in the kindergarten class. Of the six new students, two were placed at Table A and four at Table C. Thus the totals for the three tables were nine students at Table A, ten at Table B, and 14 at Table C.

The seating arrangement that began in the kindergarten emerged in the first grade as a caste phenomenon in which there was absolutely no mobility upward. That is, of those children whom Mrs. Caplow had perceived as potential "failures" and thus seated at either Table 2 or 3 in the kindergarten, not one was assigned to the table of the "fast learners" in the first grade.

The initial label given to the children by the kindergarten teacher had been reinforced in her interaction with those students throughout the school year. When the children were ready to pass into the first grade, their ascribed labels from the teacher as either successes or failures assumed objective dimensions. The first-grade teacher no longer had to rely on merely the presence or absence of certain behavioral and attitudinal characteristics to ascertain who would do well and who would do poorly in the class. Objective records of the "readiness" material completed by the children during the kindergarten year were available to her. Thus, upon the basis of what material the various tables in kindergarten had completed, Mrs. Logan could form her first-grade tables for reading and arithmetic.

The kindergarten teacher's disproportionate allocation of her teaching time had resulted in the Table 1 students' having completed more material at the end of the school year than the remainder of the class. As a result, the Table 1 group from kindergarten remained intact in the first grade, as they were the only students prepared for the first-grade reading material. Those

children from Tables 2 and 3 had to spend the first
weeks of the first-grade year finishing kindergarten level
lessons. The criteria established by the school system as
to what constituted the completion of the necessary
readiness material to begin first-grade lessons insured
that the Table 2 and 3 students could not be placed at
Table A.

It would be somewhat misleading, however, to
indicate that there was absolutely no mobility for any
of the students between the seating assignments in
kindergarten and those in the first grade. All of the
students save one who had been seated at Table 3 during
the kindergarten year were moved "up" to Table B in
the first grade. The majority of Table C students were
those having to repeat the grade level. As a tentative
explanation of Mrs. Logan's rationale for the development of the Table C seating assignments, she may have
assumed that within her class there existed one group of
students who possessed so very little of the perceived
behavioral patterns and attitudes necessary for success
that they had to be kept separate from the remainder of
the class. (Table C was placed by itself on the opposite
side of the room from Tables A and B.) The Table C
students were spoken of by the first-grade teacher in a
manner reminiscent of the way in which Mrs. Caplow
spoke of the Table 3 students the previous year.

A basic tenet in explaining Mrs. Logan's seating
arrangement is, of course, that she shared a similar
reference group and set of values as to what constitutes
"success" with Mrs. Caplow in the kindergarten class.
Both women were well educated, were employed in a
professional occupation, lived in middle-income
neighborhoods, were active in a number of charitable
and civil rights organizations and expressed strong

religious convictions and moral standards. Both were educated in the city teacher's college and had also attained graduate degrees. Their backgrounds as well as the manner in which they described the various groups of students in their classes would indicate that they shared a similar reference group and set of expectations as to what constituted the indices of the "successful" student.

Second Grade

Of the original 30 students in kindergarten and 18 in first grade, ten students were assigned to the only second-grade class in the main building. Of the eight original kindergarten students who did not come to the second grade from the first, three were repeating first grade while the remainder had moved. The teacher in the second grade also divided the class into three groups, though she did not give the number or letter designations. Rather, she called the first group the "Tigers." The middle group she labeled the "Cardinals," while the second-grade repeaters plus several new children assigned to the third table were designated by the teacher as "Clowns." The names were not given to the groups until the third week of school, though the seating arrangement was established on the third day.

In the second-grade seating scheme, no student from the first grade who had not sat at Table A was moved "up" to the Tigers at the beginning of second grade. All those students who in first grade had been at Table B or Table C and returned to the second grade were placed in the Cardinal group. The Clowns consisted of six second-grade repeaters plus three students who were new to the class. Of the ten original kindergarten students who came from the first grade, six were Tigers and four were Cardinals. Table 2 illustrates that the distribution of socioeconomic factors from the kindergarten year remained essentially unchanged in the second grade.

By the time the children came to the second grade, their seating arrangement appeared to be based not on the teacher's expectations of how the child might perform, but rather on the basis of past performance of the child. Available to the teacher when she formulated the seating groups were grade sheets from both kindergarten and first grade, IQ scores from kindergarten, listing of parental occupations for approximately half of the class, reading scores from a test given to all students at the end of the first grade, evaluations from the speech teacher and also the informal evaluations from both the kindergarten and first-grade teachers.

The single most important data utilized by the teacher in devising seating groups were the reading scores indicating the performance of the students at the end of the first grade. The second-grade teacher indicated that she attempted to divide the groups primarily on the basis of these scores. The Tigers were designated as the highest reading group and the Cardinals the middle. The Clowns were assigned a first-grade reading level, though they were, for the most part, repeaters from the previous year in second grade. The caste character of the reading groups became clear as the year progressed, in that all three groups were reading in different books and it was school policy that no child could go on to a new book until the previous one had been completed. Thus there was no way for the child, should he have demonstrated competence at a higher reading level, to advance, since he had to continue at the pace of the rest of his reading group. The teacher never

TABLE 2: Distribution of Socioeconomic Status Factors by Seating Arrangement in the Three Reading Groups in the Second-Grade Classroom.

Factors		Seating Arrangement*	
	Tigers	Cardinals	Clowns
Income			
1) Families on welfare	2	4	7
2) Families with father employed	8	5	1
3) Families with mother employed	7	11	6
4) Families with both parents employed	7	5	1
5) Total family income below $3,000. /yr**	1	5	8
6) Total family income above $12,000. /yr**	4	0	0
Education			
1) Father ever grade school	8	6	1
2) Father ever high school	7	4	0
3) Father ever college	0	0	0
4) Mother ever grade school	12	13	9
5) Mother ever high school	9	7	4
6) Mother ever college	3	0	0
7) Children with pre-school experience	1	0	0
Family Size			
1) Families with one child	2	0	1
2) Families with six or more children	3	8	5
3) Average number of siblings in family	3-4	6-7	7-8
4) Families with both parents present	8	6	1

*There are twelve children in the Tiger group, fourteen children in the Cardinal group, and nine children in the clown group.

**Estimated from stated occupation.

allowed individual reading in order that a child might finish a book on his own and move ahead. No matter how well a child in the lower reading groups might have read, he was destined to remain in the same reading group. This is, in a sense, another manifestation of the self-fulfilling prohpecy in that a "slow learner" had no option but to continue to be a slow learner, regardless of performance or potential. Initial expectations of the kindergarten teacher two years earlier as to the ability of the child resulted in placement in a reading group, whether high or low, from which there appeared to be no escape. The child's journey through the early grades of school at one reading level and in one social grouping appeared to be pre-ordained from the eighth day of kindergarten.

The expectations of the kindergarten teacher appeared to be fulfilled by late spring. Her description of the academic performance of the children in June had a strong "goodness of fit" with her stated expectations from the previous September. For the first- and second-grade teachers alike, there was no need to rely on intuitive expectations as to what the performance of the child would be. They were in the position of being able to base future expectations upon past performance. At this point, the relevance of the self-fulfilling prophecy again is evident, for the very criteria by which the first- and second-grade teachers established their three reading groups were those manifestations of performance most affected by the previous experience of the child. That is, which reading books were completed, the amount of arithmetic and reading readiness material that had been completed and the mastery of basic printing skills all became the significant criteria established by the Board of Education to determine the level at which the child would begin the first grade. A similar process of standard evaluation by past performance on criteria established by the Board appears to have been the basis for the arrangement of reading groups within the second grade. Thus, again, the initial patterns of expectations and her acting upon them appeared to place the kindergarten teacher in the position of establishing the parameters of the educational experience for the various children in her class. The parameters, most clearly defined by the seating arrangement at the various tables, remained intact through both the first and second grades.

When the second-grade teacher was asked to evaluate the children in her class by reading group, she responded in terms reminiscent of the kindergarten teacher. Though such a proposition would be tenuous at best, the high degree of similarity in the responses of both the kindergarten and second-grade teachers suggests that there may be among the teachers in the school a common set of criteria as to what constitutes the successful and promising student. If such is the case, then the particular individual who happens to occupy the role of kindergarten teacher is less crucial. For if the expectations of all staff within the school are highly similar, then with little difficulty there could be an interchange of teachers among the grades with little or no noticeable effect upon the performance of the various groups of students. If all teachers have similar expectations as to which types of students perform well and which types perform poorly, the categories established by the kindergarten teacher could be expected to reflect rather closely the manner in which other teachers would also have grouped the class.

Throughout the length of the study in the school, it

was evident that both the kindergarten and second-grade teachers were teaching the groups within their classes in a dissimilar manner. Variations were evident, for example, in the amount of time the teachers spent teaching the different groups, in the manner in which certain groups were granted privileges which were denied to others, and in the teacher's proximity to the different groups. Two additional considerations related to the teacher's use of reward and punishment.

When observations were being conducted in the second grade, it appeared that there was on the part of Mrs. Benson a differentiation of reward and punishment similar to that displayed by Mrs. Caplow. In order to examine more closely the degree to which variations were present over time, three observational periods were totally devoted to the tabulation of each of the individual behavioral units directed by the teacher towards the children. Each observational period was three and one-half hours in length, lasting from 8:30 A.M. to 12:00 noon.

A mechanism for evaluating the varieties of teacher behavior was developed. Behavior on the part of the teacher was tabluated as "behavioral unit" when there was clearly directed towards an individual child some manner of communication, whether it be verbal, non-verbal or physical contact. When, within the interaction of the teacher and the student, there occurred more than one type of behavior, i.e., the teacher spoke to the child and touched him, a count was made of both variations. The following is a list of the nine variations in teacher behavior that were tabulated within the second-grade classroom. Several examples are also included with each of the alternatives displayed by the teacher within the class.

1) Verbal Supportive—"That's a very good job." "You are such a lovely girl." "My, but your work is so neat."

2) Verbal Neutral—"Laura and Tom, let's open our books to page 34." "May, your pencil is on the floor." "Hal, do you have milk money today?"

3) Verbal Control—"Lou, sit on that chair and shut up." "Curt, get up off that floor." "Mary and Laura, quit your talking."

4) Non-verbal Supportive—Teacher nods her head at Rose. Teacher smiles at Liza. Teacher claps when Laura completes her problem at the board.

5) Non-verbal Neutral—Teacher indicates with her arms that she wants Lilly and Shirley to move farther apart in the circle. Teacher motions to Joe and Tom that they should try to snap their fingers to stay in beat with the music.

6) Non-verbal Control—Teacher frowns at Lena. Teacher shakes finger at Amy to quit tapping her pencil. Teacher motions with hand for Rose not to come to her desk.

7) Physical Contact Supportive—Teacher hugs Laura. Teacher places her arm around Mary as she talks to her. Teacher holds Trish's hand as she takes out a splinter.

8) Physical Contact Neutral—Teacher touches head of Nick as she walks past. Teacher leads Rema to new place on the circle.

9) Physical Contact Control—Teacher strikes Lou with stick. Teacher pushes Curt down in his chair. Teacher pushes Hal and Doug to the floor.

Table 3 presents all forms of control, supportive and neutral behavior grouped together within each of the three observational periods. Since the categorization of

the various types of behavior was decided as the
interaction occurred and there was no cross-validation
checks by another observer, all behavior was placed in
the appropriate neutral category which could not be
clearly distinguished as belonging to one of the established supportive or control categories. This may explain
the large percentage of neutral behavior tabulated in
each of the three observational periods.

The picture of the second-grade teacher, Mrs. Benson,
that emerges from analysis of these data is of one who
distributes rewards quite sparingly and equally, but who
utilizes somewhere between two and five times as much
control-oriented behavior with the Clowns as with the
Tigers. With the Tigers the combination of neutral and
supportive behavior never dropped below 93 percent of
the total behavior directed towards them by the teacher
in the three periods; the lowest figure for the Cardinals
was 86 percent and for the Clowns, 73 percent. It may
be assumed that neutral and supportive behavior would
be conducive to learning while punishment or control-
oriented behavior would not. Thus for the Tigers, the
learning situation was one with only infrequent units of
control, while for the Clowns, control behavior constituted one-fourth of all behavior directed towards them
on at least one occasion.

Studies have indicated that children within an authoritarian classroom display a decrease in both learning and
retention and performance, while those within the
democratic classroom do not. In extrapolating these
findings to the second-grade classroom of Mrs. Benson,
one cannot say that she was continually "authoritarian"
as opposed to "democratic" with her students, but that
with one group of students there occurred more
control-oriented behavior than with other groups. On at

TABLE 3: Variations in Teacher-Directed Behavior for Three Second Grade Reading Groups During Three Observational Periods Within a Single Classroom.

Item	Variations in Teacher-Directed Behavior		
	Control	Supportive	Neutral
Observational Period 1*			
Tigers	5%—(6)**	7%—(8)	87%—(95)
Cardinals	10%—(7)	8%—(5)	82%—(58)
Clowns	27%—(27)	6%—(6)	67%—(67)
Observational Period 2			
Tigers	7%—(14)	8%—(16)	85%—(170)
Cardinals	7%—(13)	8%—(16)	85%—(157)
Clowns	14%—(44)	6%—(15)	80%—(180)
Observational Period 3			
Tigers	7%—(15)	6%—(13)	86%—(171)
Cardinals	14%—(20)	10%—(14)	75%—(108)
Clowns	15%—(36)	7%—(16)	78%—(188)

*Forty-eight (48) minutes of unequal teacher access (due to one group of children's being out of the room) was eliminated from the analysis.

**Value within the parentheses indicates total number of units of behavior within that category.

least one occasion Mrs. Benson utilized nearly five times the amount of control-oriented behavior with the Clowns as with her perceived high-interest and high-ability group, the Tigers. For the Clowns, who were most isolated from the teacher and received the least amount of her teaching time, the results noted above would indicate that the substantial control-oriented behavior directed towards them would compound their difficulty in experiencing significant learning and cognitive growth.

Here discussion of the self-fulfilling prophecy is relevant: given the extent to which the teacher utilized control-oriented behavior with the Clowns, data from the leadership and performance studies would indicate that it would be more difficult for that group to experience a positive learning situation. The question remains unanswered, though, as to whether the behavior of uninterested students necessitated the teacher's resorting to extensive use of control-oriented behavior, or whether that to the extent to which the teacher utilized control-oriented behavior, the students responded with uninterest. If the prior experience of the Clowns was in any way similar to that of the students in kindergarten at Table 3 and Table C in the first grade, I am inclined to opt for the latter proposition.

A very serious and, I believe, justifiable consequence of this assumption of student uninterest related to the frequency of the teacher's control-oriented behavior is that the teachers themselves contribute significantly to the creation of the "slow learners" within their classrooms. Over time, this may help account for the phenomenon noted in the Coleman Report (1966) that the gap between the academic performance of the disadvantaged students and national norms increased the longer the students remained in the school system. During one of the three and one-half hour observational periods in the second grade, the percentage of control-oriented behavior directed toward the entire class was about 8 percent. Of the behavior directed toward the Clowns, however, 27 percent was control-oriented behavior—more than three times the amount of control-oriented behavior directed to the class as a whole.

On another level, the teacher's use of control-oriented behavior is directly related to the expectations of the ability and willingness of "slow learners" to learn the material she teaches. That is, if the student is uninterested in what goes on in the classroom, he is more apt to engage in activities that the teacher perceives as disruptive. Activities such as talking out loud, coloring when the teacher has not said it to be permissible, attempting to leave the room, calling other students' attention to activities occurring on the street, making comments to the teacher not pertinent to the lesson, dropping books, falling out of the chair and commenting on how the student cannot wait for recess, all prompt the teacher to employ control-oriented behavior towards that student. The interactional pattern between the uninterested student and the teacher literally becomes a "vicious circle" in which control-oriented behavior is followed by further manifestations of uninterest, followed by further control behavior and so on. The stronger the reciprocity of this pattern of interaction, the greater one may anticipate the strengthening of the teacher's expectation of the "slow learner" as being either unable or unwilling to learn.

The placement of the children within the various classrooms into different reading groups was ostensibly done on the promise of future performance in the kindergarten and on differentials of past performance in later grades. However, the placement may rather have been done from purely irrational reasons that had nothing to do with academic performance. The utilization of academic criteria may have served as the rationalization for a more fundamental process occurring with the class whereby the teacher served as the agent of the larger society to ensure that proper "social distance" was maintained between the various strata of the society as represented by the children.

Within the context of this analysis there appear to be at least two interactional processes that may be identified as having occurred simultaneously within the kindergarten classroom. The first was the relation of the teacher to the students placed at Table 1. The process appeared to occur in at least four stages. The initial stage involved the kindergarten teacher's developing expectations regarding certain students as possessing a series of characteristics that she considered essential for future academic "success." Second, the teacher reinforced through her mechanisms of "positive" differential behavior those characteristics of the children that she considered important and desirable.

Third, the children responded with more of the behavior that initially gained them the attention and support of the teacher. Perceiving that verbalization, for example, was a quality that the teacher appeared to admire, the Table 1 children increased their level of verbalization throughout the school year. Fourth, the cycle was complete as the teacher focused even more specifically on the children at Table 1 who continued to manifest the behavior she desired. A positive interactional scheme arose whereby initial behavioral patterns of the student were reinforced into apparent permanent behavioral patterns, once he had received support and differential treatment from the teacher.

The actual academic potential of the students was not objectively measured prior to the kindergarten teacher's evaluation of expected performance. The students may be assumed to have had mixed potential. However, the common positive treatment accorded to all within the group by the teacher may have served as the necessary catalyst for the self-fulfilling prophecy whereby those expected to do well did so.

A concurrent behavioral process appeared to occur between the teacher and those students placed at Tables 2 and 3. The student came into the class possessing a series of behavioral and attitudinal characteristics that within the frame of reference to the teacher were perceived as indicative of "failure." Second, through mechanisms of reinforcement of her initial expectations as to the future performance of the student, it was made evident that he was not perceived as similar or equal to those at the table of fast learners. In the third stage, the student responded to both the definition and actual treatment given to him by the teacher which emphasized his characteristics of being an educational "failure." Given the high degree of control-oriented behavior directed towards the "slower" learner, the lack of verbal interaction and encouragement, the disproportionally small amount of teaching time given to him, and the ridicule and hostility, the child withdrew from class participation. The fourth stage was the cyclical repetition of behavioral and attitudinal characteristics that led to the initial labelling as an educational failure.

As with those perceived as having high probability of future success, the academic potential of the failure group was not objectively determined prior to evaluation by the kindergarten teacher. This group also may be assumed to have come into the class with mixed potential. Some within the group may have had the capacity to perform academic tasks quite well, while others perhaps did not. Yet the reinforcement by the teacher of the characteristics in the children that she had perceived as leading to academic failure may, in fact, have created the very conditions of student failure. With the "negative" treatment accorded to the perceived failure group, the teacher's definition of the situation may have ensured its emergence. What the teacher perceived in the children may have served as the catalyst for a series of interactions, with the result that the child came to act out within the class the very expectations defined for him by the teacher.

As an alternative explanation, however, the teacher may have developed the system of caste segregation within the classroom, not because the groups of children were so dissimilar they had to be handled in an entirely different manner, but because they were, in fact, so very close to one another. The teacher may have believed quite strongly that the ghetto community inhibited the development of middle-class models. Thus, it was her duty to "save" at least one group of children from the "streets." Those children had to be kept separate who could have had a bad influence on the children who appeared to have a chance to make it in the middle class of the larger society. Within this framework, the teacher's actions may be understood not only as an attempt to keep the slow learners away from those fast learners, but to ensure that the fast learners would not so be influenced that they themselves become enticed with the streets and lose their apparent opportunity for future middle-class status.

Given the extreme intercomplexity of the organizational structure of this society, the institutions that both create and sustain social organization can neither be held singularly responsible for perpetuating the inequalities nor for eradicating them. The public school system, I believe, is justifiably responsible for contributing to the present structure of the society, but the responsibility is not its alone. The picture that emerges from this study is that the school strongly shares in the complicity of maintaining the organizational perpetuation of poverty and unequal opportunity. This, of course, is in contrast to the formal doctrine of education in this country to ameliorate rather than aggravate the conditions of the poor.

The teachers' reliance on a mixed black-white middle class for their normative reference group appeared to contain assumptions of superiority over those of lower-class and status positions. For they and those members of their reference group, comfortable affluence, education, community participation and possession of professional status may have afforded a rather stable view of the social order. The treatment of those from lower socioeconomic backgrounds within the classrooms by the teachers may have indicated that the values highly esteemed by them were not open to members of the lower groups. Thus the lower groups were in numerous ways informed of their lower status and were socialized for a role of lower self expectations and also for respect and deference towards those of higher status. The social distance between the groups within the classrooms was manifested in its extreme form by the maintenance of patterns of caste segregation whereby those of lower positions were not allowed to become a part of the peer group at the highest level. The value system of the teachers appeared to necessitate that a certain group be ostracized due to "unworthiness" or inherent inferiority. The very beliefs which legitimated exclusion were maintained among those of the higher social group which then contributed to the continuation of the pattern of social organization itself.

It has not been a contention of this study that the teachers observed could not or would not teach their students. They did, I believe, teach quite well. But the high quality teaching was not made equally accessible to all students in the class. For the students of high socioeconomic background who were perceived by the teachers as possessing desirable behavioral and attitudinal characteristics, the classroom experience was one where the teachers displayed interest in them, spent a large proportion of teaching time with them, directed little control-oriented behavior towards them, held them as models for the remainder of the class and continually reinforced statements that they were "special" students. If the classrooms observed had contained only those students perceived by the teachers as having a desirable social status and a high probability of future success outside the confines of the ghetto community, the teachers could be assumed to have continued to teach well, and under these circumstances, to the entire class.

Though this analysis has focused on the early years of schooling for a single group of black children attending a ghetto school, the implications are far-reaching for those situations where there are children from different status backgrounds within the same classroom. When a teacher bases her expectations of performance on the social status of the student and assumes that the higher the social status, the higher the potential of the child, those children of low social status suffer a stigmatization outside of their own choice or will. Yet there is a greater tragedy than being labeled as a slow learner, and that is being treated as one. The differential amounts of control-oriented behavior, the lack of interaction with the teacher, the ridicule from one's peers and the caste aspects of being placed in lower reading groups all have implications for the future life style and value of education for the child.

The success of an educational institution and any individual teacher should not be measured by the treatment of the high-achieving students, but rather by the treatment of those not achieving. As is the case with a chain, ultimate value is based on the weakest member. So long as the lower-status students are treated differently in both quality and quantity of education, there will exist an imperative for change.

It should be apparent, of course, that if one desires this society to retain its present social class configuration and the disproportional access to wealth, power, social and economic mobility, medical care and choice of life styles, one should not disturb the methods of education as presented in this study. This contention is made because what develops as "caste" within the classrooms appears to emerge in the larger society as "class." The low-income children segregated as a caste of "unclean and intellectually inferior" persons may very well be those who in their adult years become the car washers, dishwashers, welfare recipients and participants in numerous other un- or underemployed roles within this society. The question may quite honestly be asked, "Given the treatment of low-income children from the beginning of their kindergarten experience, for what class strata are they being prepared other than that of the lower class?" It appears that the public school system not only mirrors the configurations of the larger society, but also significantly contributes to maintaining them. Thus the system of public education in reality perpetuates what it is ideologically committed to eradicate—class barriers which result in inequality in the social and economic life of the citizenry.

FURTHER READING:

The Disadvantaged Child edited by M. Deutsch, *et al* (New York: Basic Books, 1967).

Life in Classrooms by P. Jackson, (New York: Holt, Rinehart & Winston, 1968).

Teaching and Learning in City Schools by E. Leacock, (New York: Basic Books, 1969).

Pygmalion in the Classroom by Lenore Jacobson and R. Rosenthal, (New York: Holt, Rinehart & Winston, 1968).

The Complexities of an Urban Classroom by W. Geoffrey and L. Smith, (New York: Holt, Rinehart & Winston, 1968).

CREATIVITY
AND INTELLIGENCE

Part III.

Creativity and Intelligence
in Children

MICHAEL A. WALLACH and NATHAN KOGAN

While there has been a great deal of discussion in recent years concerning the importance of fostering "creativity" in our children, there is little solid evidence to support the claim that creativity can be distinguished from the more familiar concept of intelligence. To be sure, the word "creativity" has caught the fancy of the culture—frequent reference is made to creativity in contexts as diverse as education, industry and advertising. Time and time again, however, the "proof" offered to support the existence of a type of cognitive excellence different from general intelligence has proven to be a will-o-the-wisp.

The logical requirements for such a proof can be put as follows. The psychological concept of *intelligence* defines a network of strongly related abilities concerning the retention, transformation and utilization of verbal and numerical symbols: at issue are a person's memory storage capacities, his skill in solving problems, his dexterity in manipulating and dealing with concepts. The person high in one of these skills will tend to be high in all; the individual who is low in one will tend to be low in all. But what of the psychological concept of *creativity?* If the behavior judged to be indicative of creativity turns up in the same persons who behave in the ways we call "intelligent," then there is no justification for claiming the existence of any kind of cognitive capacity apart from general intelligence. We would have to assert that the notion of greater or lesser degrees of *creativity* in people simply boils down, upon empirical inspection, to the notion of greater or lesser degrees of general *intelligence.* On the other hand, in order to demonstrate that there are grounds for considering creativity to be a kind of cognitive talent that exists in its own right, another kind of proof would be required. It would be necessary to demonstrate that whatever methods of evaluation are utilized to define variations in creativity from person to person result in classifications that are different from those obtained when the same individuals are categorized as to intelligence.

When we reviewed the quantitative research on creativity, we were forced to conclude that these logical requirements were not met. Despite frequent use of the term "creativity" to define a form of talent that was independent of intelligence, examination of the evidence indicated that the purported measures of creativity tended to have little more in common with each other than they had in common with measures of general intelligence. If one could do about the same thing with an IQ measure as one could with the creativity measures (regarding who should be considered more creative and who should be considered less creative), it was difficult to defend the practice of invoking a new and glamorous term such as "creativity" for describing the kind of talent under study.

While varying conceptions of the meaning of creativity had been embodied in the measures used, they all shared one thing in common: they had been administered to the persons under study as *tests*. From the viewpoint of the person undergoing assessment, the creativity procedures, no less than an intelligence test, carried the aura of school examinations. They were carried out with explicit or implicit time limits in classroom settings where many students underwent the assessment procedures at the same time. Indeed, we even found that the creativity procedures had been described to the students as "tests" by the psychologists who gave them.

We were suspicious that such a test-like context was inimical to the wholehearted display of cognitive characteristics which could be correctly referred to as being involved in creativity. Hence we believed that creativity had not yet been given a fair chance to reveal itself as a different form of excellence than intelligence. These suspicions were reinforced when we considered what creative artists and scientists have said concerning creative moments in their own work.

In their introspections one finds an emphasis upon the production of a free flow of ideas—the bubbling forth of varieties of associations concerning the matter at hand. Einstein, for example, refers to the need for "combinatory play" and "associative play" in putting ideas together. Dryden describes the process of writing as involving "a confus'd mass of thoughts, tumbling over one another in the dark." Poincaré talks about ideas as having "rose in crowds" immediately prior to his obtaining a significant mathematical insight. These associations, moreover, range with high frequency into the consideration of unique, unusual possibilities, but ones which are nevertheless relevant to the issue rather than just bizarre. When we look into the conditions under which an abundant flow of unique ideational possibilities has been available, the artists and scientists indicate that the most conducive attitude is one of playful contemplation—if you will, of permissiveness. Creative awareness tends to occur when the individual— in a playful manner—entertains a range of possibilities without worry concerning his own personal success or failure and how his self-image will fare in the eyes of others.

With this in mind we formulated a research program that involved the extensive study of 151 fifth-grade children. They were of middle-class socioeconomic status, and boys and girls were about equally represented in our sample. The work, which was supported in part by the Cooperative Research Program of the United States Office of Education, has been described in detail in our book, *Modes of Thinking in Young Children: A Study of the Creativity-Intelligence Distinction.*

From the introspections of scientists and artists arose some ground rules concerning what creativity might rightfully signify if in fact it constitutes a type of excellence different from intelligence. These ground rules might be put in terms of the following two injunctions:

☐ First, study the flow of ideas—consider how unique and how abundant are the kinds of ideas that a child can provide when contemplating various sorts of tasks. One is talking here, of course, about relevant ideas, not about ideas that might earn the status of being unique only because they are so bizarre as to have no relevance at all to the task.

□ Second, provide an atmosphere that convinces the child that he is not under test—that the situation is one of play rather than one where his intellectual worthiness is under evaluation by others. This second injunction may be a particularly difficult one to fulfill on the American educational scene, where testing and the feeling of undergoing personal evaluation are ubiquitous. Yet if our considerations were correct, it obviously was essential to fulfill it if creativity was to receive a fighting chance to display itself.

Accordingly, we mustered every device possible to place the assessment procedures in a context of play rather than in the typical context of testing with which the children were all too familiar. There were no time limits on the procedures. They were administered to one child at a time rather than to groups of children seated at their classroom desks. The adults who worked with the children, moreover, had already established relationships in the context of play activities. We even took pains to avoid the customary vocabulary of tests and testing in connection with the research enterprise as a whole—in our talk with the children we described the work as oriented to the study of children's games for purposes of developing new games children would like.

The procedures involved such matters as requesting the child to suggest possible uses for each of several objects, or to describe possible ways in which each of several pairs of objects are similar to each other. For example, in one procedure the child was to suggest all the different ways in which we could use such objects as a newspaper, a cork, a shoe, a chair. "Rip it up if angry" was a unique response for "newspáper," while "make paper hats" was not unique. In another, he was to indicate similarities between, for example, a potato and a carrot, a cat and a mouse, milk and meat. "They are government-inspected" was a unique response for "milk and meat," while "they come from animals" was not unique. In yet another, he was to indicate all the things that each of a number of abstract drawings might be—such as the drawings shown in the illustrations. For the triangle with three circles around it, "three mice eating a piece of cheese" was a unique response, while "three people sitting around a table" was not unique. For the two half-circles over the line, "two haystacks on a flying carpet" was a unique response, while "two igloos" was not unique.

Our interests were in the number of ideas that a child would suggest, and the uniqueness of the suggested ideas—the extent to which a given idea in response to a given task belonged to one child alone rather than being an idea that was suggested by other children as well. In addition, we used a variety of traditional techniques for assessing general intelligence with the same children.

When the results of the creativity assessment procedures were compared with the results of the intelli-

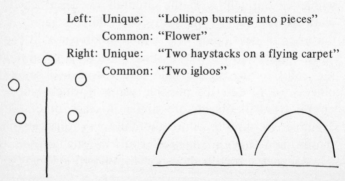

Left: Unique: "Lollipop bursting into pieces"
        Common: "Flower"
Right: Unique: "Two haystacks on a flying carpet"
        Common: "Two igloos"

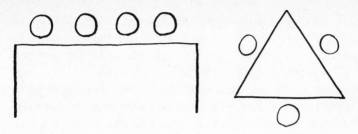

CHILDREN'S RESPONSES TO ABSTRACT DRAWINGS

Left: Unique: "Foot and Toes"
           Common: "Table with things on top"
Right: Unique: "Three mice eating a piece of cheese"
           Common: "Three people sitting around a table"

gence measures, a definite divergence was obtained—the kind that had not been found in earlier studies. They had already shown, and so did our study, that a child who scores at the high intelligence end of one intelligence test will tend to score that way in other intelligence tests as well. In addition, however, our research revealed two further facts which tended to be different from earlier studies:

☐ The various measures of creativity that we utilized had a great deal in common with one another: a child who scored at the high creativity end of one of our creativity measures tended to score at the high creativity end of all the rest of these measures.

☐ Of particular importance, the indices of creativity and the indices of intelligence tended to be independent of each other. That is to say, a child who was creative by our measures would just as likely be of low intelligence as of high intelligence. Likewise, a child who was relatively low in creativity by our measures would as likely be of high intelligence as of low intelligence.

In short, the obtained facts *did* support the view that

in school children creativity is a different type of cognitive excellence than general intelligence. Such an outcome was especially striking in light of the fact that our procedures for assessing creativity of necessity called upon the child's verbal ability in some degree— and verbal ability is known to contribute substantially to performance on IQ tests. Despite this possible source of commonality, the chances that a child of high intelligence would also display high creativity by our measures were no more than about 50-50.

What are some of the characteristics, then, of children in our four categories: intelligent and creative; neither intelligent nor creative; intelligent but low in creativity; and creative but low in regard to intelligence? The composite pictures that emerged from the experiments and observations that we carried out are composites in the sense that some portions of the evidence upon which they are based were more clear for the boys, while other parts of the evidence were more clear for the girls. However, the general pictures that emerged for the two sexes tended to suggest the same underlying characteristics.

High creativity—High intelligence: In many respects these children earn the most superlatives of any of the four groups. For example, when they are observed in the classroom they tend to be particularly high in degree of attention span and concentration upon academic work. At the same time, their academic bent does not put them at a social disadvantage. Quite to the contrary, they are observed to be the most socially "healthy" of the four groups: they have the strongest inclination to be friends with others, and others also have the strongest inclination to be friends with them. (These observations were made during play periods as well as during class sessions.)

These children, in addition, are the least likely of all four groups to behave in ways that suggest disapproval or doubt concerning oneself, one's actions and one's work. However, this isn't merely a question of behaving in a manner most in harmony with the society's expectations, for these children also demonstrate a strong inclination to engage in various sorts of disruptive activities in the classroom. It's as if they are bursting through the typical behavioral molds that the society has constructed.

What are some of the underpinnings of the general behaviors just described for this group? For one thing, they are likely to see possible connections between events that do not have too much in common. The members of this group, in other words, are more willing to posit relationships between events that are in many respects dissimilar. For another thing, these children are particularly good at reading the subtle affective or expressive connotations that can be carried by what goes on in the environment. These two matters are not entirely separate—a sensitive, aesthetic "tuning" to the possible expressive meanings conveyed by human gesture or by abstract design forms involves seeing possible linkages between quite different kinds of objects and events. The children high in both creativity and intelligence seemed to be most capable of all the groups regarding this kind of aesthetic sensitivity.

To illustrate how we studied the child's ability to read subtle expressive connotations, consider the following example. We confronted the child with a picture of a straight line and asked him to imagine that he was looking down from above at a path that someone had made. The child was to tell us what sort of person made this trail. Our interest was in determining whether the child's response conveyed information about the kinds of emotional experience that might characterize the person in question, or on the other hand conveyed information only about the superficial character of what the person did. An example of a response showing sensitivity to possible expressive meanings was: "Someone very tense; because if he were relaxed he might wander all over; somebody mad." On the other hand, here is an example of a response that did not show expressive sensitivity: "Man was traveling on a highway; he met people in a huge car; it had a lot of people and it was crowded; they traveled together and got food in restaurants; when they got where they were going, they had a nice vacation."

Turning finally to the way these children describe their own feeling states, we find a tendency for them to admit to experiencing some anxiety, some disturbance—neither a great deal nor very little It may be that experiencing some anxiety serves an energizing function for them: it is not so much anxiety as to cripple them, and not so little anxiety as to leave them dormant. Also, their total mode of adaptation does not minimize the experience of anxiety for them.

Low creativity—High intelligence: In what respects are the children who are high with regard to general intelligence but low in creativity different from those who are high in both? Let us return first to behavior observed in classroom and play settings. While the high intelligence-low creativity children resembled the high creativity-high intelligence children in possessing strong capacities for concentration on academic work and a long attention span, in other respects they were quite different. Those of high intelligence but low creativity were least likely of all four groups to engage in disruptive activities in the classroom and tended to hesitate about expressing opinions. In short, these children seemed rather unwilling to take chances.

Parallel behavior was observed in their social relations with other children; while others had a strong inclination to be friends with them, they in turn tended to hold themselves aloof from interaction with other children. The high intelligence-low creativity children, therefore, seemed to be characterized by a coolness or reserve in relations with their peers. Others would seek out the high intelligence-low creativity children for companionship, possibly because of this group's high academic standing. The children in question, however, tended not to seek out others in return. Perhaps this group felt themselves to be on top of the social mountain, as it were—in a position where they could receive homage from others without any need for requital.

The observations regarding a tendency toward caution and reserve on the part of the high intelligence-low creativity children receive further corroboration in other areas of their functioning. For example, when asked to make arrangements and groupings of pictures of everyday objects in whatever ways they considered most suitable, they preferred to make groupings that were more conventional in nature. They tended to avoid making free-wheeling, unconventional arrangements in which there would be greater free play for evolving unique combinations of objects. For instance, a more conventional grouping would be assembling pictures of a lamppost, a door and a hammer, and calling them "hard objects." A more unconventional grouping, on the other hand, would be putting together pictures of a comb, a lipstick, a watch, a pocketbook and a door, and describing them as items that concern "getting ready to go out." It is as if a greater fear of error characterizes these children, so that when left to their own devices, they tend to gravitate toward ways of construing the world that are less open to criticism by others.

We also found out that if you request these children to try to behave in a manner that involves establishing more free-wheeling linkages among objects, they are capable of doing so. It is not that they lack the ability to look at the world in this manner, but the inclination. When an adult in their environment comes along and makes it clear that they are expected to consider unusual and possible bizarre ways in which objects can be linked, they are able to conform to this task demand with skill. But most of the time, their environment tells them that the more unconventional ways of proceeding are more likely to lead them into error and be criticized as wrong. Since the possibility of error seems particularly painful to these children, their typical behavior is to proceed in a manner that is less likely, on the average, to bring them criticism.

Another example of the same sort of process is provided when we consider how the high intelligence-low creativity group reads the possible affective meanings that can be possessed by the behavior of others. As in the case of arranging objects into groups, one can contrast more conventional, expected ways and more unconventional, unusual ways of construing what the behavior of others may signify. For example, an angry figure can be described as "angry" with little risk of error. It requires acceptance of unconventional possibilities, on the other hand, for the child to admit the idea that this figure might be "peaceful" or might be "searching." It turns out that the group in question is least likely to entertain the possibility of the more unconventional, unusual kinds of meanings. They seem locked, therefore, in more conventional ways of interpreting their social world as well as their physical world. Again, fear of possible error seems to be at work.

Since the high intelligence-low creativity children seem to behave in a manner that should maximize correctness and minimize error, we can expect them to be in particularly good standing in their classroom environment. Given their apparent tendency to conform to expectations, their mode of functioning should be maximally rewarding and minimally punishing for them. In short, there should be a high degree of fit between customary environmental expectations and their way of conducting themselves. We find, in fact, that this group admits to little anxiety or disturbance when asked to describe their own feeling states. Their self-descriptions indicate the lowest levels of anxiety reported by any of the four creativity-intelligence groups. Since this group behaves in a manner that should minimize worry or concern for them, their minimal level of reported anxiety probably represents an an accurate description of how they feel. But at a cost, as we have noted, of functioning in a constricted manner.

High creativity—Low intelligence: Turning to the group characterized by high creativity but relatively low intelligence, we find, first of all, that they tend to exhibit disruptive behavior in the classroom. This is about the only respect, however, in which their observable conduct in the usual school and play settings resembles that of the group high in both creativity and intelligence. Of all four groups, the high creativity-low intelligence children are the least able to concentrate and maintain attention in class, the lowest in self-confidence and the most likely to express the conviction that they are no good. It is as if they are convinced that their case is a hopeless one. Furthermore, they are relatively isolated socially; not only do they avoid contact with other children, but in addition their peers shun them more than any other group. Perhaps, in their social withdrawal, these children are indulging fantasy activities. At any rate, they are relatively alone in the school setting, and in many respects can be characterized as worse off than the group low in both creativity and intelligence.

It should be borne in mind that the high creativity-low intelligence children nevertheless give evidence of the same kind of creative thinking capacities as are found in the high creativity-high intelligence group. Again, for example, we find a greater likelihood of seeing possible connections between events that do not share much in common. The high creativity children, whether high or low regarding intelligence, are more willing to postulate relationships between somewhat dissimilar events.

Apparently, the kinds of evaluational pressures present in the case of intelligence and achievement testing as well as in the typical classroom environment serve to disrupt cognitive powers which can come to the fore when pressure is reduced. An interesting complementarity seems to exist with regard to the psychological situations found for the high creativity-low intelligence group and the low creativity-high intelligence group: while members of the former seem to perform more effectively when evaluational pressures are absent, members of the latter seem to work more adequately when evaluational pressures are present. It is as if the former children tend to go to pieces if questions of personal competence and achievement enter the picture, while the latter children have difficulty if they are denied a framework of standards within which they can evaluate what is required of them if they are to seem competent in the eyes of adults.

Low creativity—Low intelligence: While the children in this group show the greatest cognitive deprivation of the four groups under study, they seem to make up for it at least to some degree in the social sphere. From observations of their behavior in school and at play they are found to be more extroverted socially, less hesitant, and more self-confident and self-assured than the children of low intelligence but high creativity. The members of the low-low group are particularly poor regarding the kinds of aesthetic sensitivity that were mentioned earlier—for example, they show the weakest tendencies to respond to the possible expressive meanings that abstract line forms may convey. Despite such deficiencies, however, this group does not seem to be the maximally disadvantaged group in the classroom. Rather, the low-low children seem to have worked out a *modus vivendi* that puts them at greater social ease in the school situation than is the case for their high creativity-low intelligence peers.

Now that we have characterized the four groups of children, let us finally consider the implications of the relative roles played by ability and by motivational factors in a child's thinking. The only group that looks like it is in difficulty with regard to ability—and even in their case we cannot be sure—is the group low in both intelligence and creativity. In the cases of the two groups that are low regarding one cognitive skill and high regarding the other—the low intelligence-high creativity group and the high intelligence-low creativity group—our evidence suggests that, rather than an ability deficiency, the children in question are handicapped by particular motivational dispositions receiving strong environmental support. For the low intelligence-high creativity children, the difficulty seems to concern excessive fear of being evaluated; hence they perform poorly when evaluational standards are a prominent part of the setting. For the high intelligence-low creativity children, on the other hand, the difficulty seems to concern a fear of not knowing whether one is thought well of by significant others. The possibility of making mistakes, therefore, is particularly avoided. Further, if evaluational standards are not a clear part of the setting, so that the child does not know a right way of behaving in order to fulfill the expectations of others, performance will deteriorate because the problem of avoiding error becomes of prime importance.

In theory, at least, these kinds of motivational hindrances could be rectified by appropriate training procedures. If one could induce the low intelligence-high creativity children to be less concerned when evaluational standards are present, and the high intelligence-low creativity children to be less concerned when evaluational standards are absent, their thinking behavior might come to display high levels of both intelligence and creativity.

January/February 1967

FURTHER READING:

Creativity and Intelligence: Explorations With Gifted Students, by Jacob W. Getzels and Philip W. Jackson (New York: Wiley, 1962).

Guiding Creative Talent, by E. Paul Torrance (Englewood Cliffs, N.J.: Prentice-Hall, 1962).

Modes of Thinking in Young Children: A Study of the Creativity-Intelligence Distinction, by Michael A. Wallach and Nathan Kogan (New York: Holt, Rinehart and Winston, 1965).

The Talented Student, by M.A. Wallach and C.W. Wing, Jr. (New York: Holt, Rinehart and Winston, 1969).

"Creativity" by M.A. Wallach, in P.H. Mussen (Ed.), *Carmichael's Manual of Child Psychology,* 3rd ed., Vol. 1. (New York: Wiley, 1970).

College Admissions and the Psychology of Talent, by C.W. Wing, Jr., and M.A. Wallach (New York: Holt, Rinehart and Winston, 1971).

The Creative Artist
as an Explorer

JACOB W. GETZELS
and
MIHALY CSIKSZENTMIHALYI

"All good things which exist," said John Stuart Mill, "are the fruits of originality." An overstatement perhaps, but an accurate reflection of the special value that Western man since the Renaissance has placed on creative imagination. Few qualities have been so widely praised; and few have been so little understood. Popular mythology has alternately endowed the creative man with the muse, divine inspiration, pathological excesses of temperament, and, occasionally, an uncommon supply of intelligence and good sense.

What do we know about creativity itself? So far, most of the answers have been indirect. Researchers have concentrated on describing creativity in terms of the common personality characteristics the creative person possesses: Is he outgoing, or introverted? Is he easygoing, or tense? Are his values the same as those of most people, or different? The answers to questions of this sort have helped us develop at least a fragmentary and tentative model of what the creative man is like. But they told us almost nothing about what he does when he is creating—what actually happens when he sits down at the piano, or the typewriter or the sketch pad.

We have now begun to find some of the answers, specifically for the artist, by observing him in the act of creation. We studied 200 young artists who were, for the most part, still students at one of the leading art schools in the country. Some of them were already winning prizes in competitive shows, exhibiting in professional galleries, or supporting themselves on the proceeds of their illustrating skills. (We felt that our subjects deserved to be called "artists" because of their success in an art school of the highest professional standards and for their perseverance in pursuit of an artistic career, sometimes at considerable personal sacrifice.)

With the exception of those few whose work becomes fashionable among wealthy patrons and collectors, most artists, because they make so little money, are failures by the standards of society as a whole. What compensation does the artist get to make this precarious life worthwhile and even compelling? Part of the answer is in his values.

We compared our 200 art students with a cross-section of the college population to see how the value orientations of the two groups might differ on six standard dimensions: the economic, aesthetic, social, political, theoretical and religious. The results were striking. While economic values were close to the top for the average male college student, the art student ranked them close to the bottom. The only value for which the art students had less apparent respect, in fact, was the social.

But before expanding on this point, let us consider the positive side of the artist's value orientation. The most notable was the artist's extreme adherence to the aesthetic value. This in itself was not surprising—we had expected the art students to show a much stronger interest in aesthetic values than the other students did. But what startled us was the single-mindedness of this commitment. Nothing but art really seemed to matter to them. The point is not that artists' aesthetic values were so high—the religious values of clergymen are also high—but that they were so high in proportion to all other values.

Second to the aesthetic—and considerably below it in importance—came the theoretical. The aesthetic and theoretical value orientations were once thought to be mutually exclusive. The dominant interest of the theoretical man is the discovery of truth. He divests himself of judgments regarding the beauty of objects, and seeks only to observe and to reason. The aesthetic attitude is, in a sense, diametrically opposed to the theoretical. The former is concerned with the diversity, the latter with the identity of experience. The aesthetic man either equates beauty with truth, or may hold that beauty is more important than truth. Recent studies have shown, however, that creative persons in several other professions, like our artists, hold both high aesthetic and high theoretical values, and the conjunction of these values may well provide us with a useful clue as to the nature of the creative process itself.

When we categorized the art students by their fields of specialization, definite differences in the value pattern appeared. The fine arts students showed markedly different value patterns from the students planning to go into commercial and advertising art. The fine arts group showed the most extreme and exclusive adherence to aesthetic values, while the advertising art students showed value patterns more like those of the average college student. There is a great difference in values between people whose main goal is to produce work satisfying their own requirements and those whose goal is to satisfy the demands imposed by an advertising agency or a design studio.

Returning to the artists' (and particularly those in the fine arts) lack of interest in economic and social values, we can see that these students are psychologically well prepared for the conditions that their chosen career will offer. Artists are likely to be poor, at least until they get their "break" and perhaps permanently if that break never comes; they are likely to be lonely because so few people will share their interests, attitudes and values; and they are likely to be disapproved or even rejected by the people of the larger society simply because they are "different." Does all this matter to them? Apparently not. In fact, to stand outside the distracting scramble of everyday business may even be an asset if a man is to devote his energies almost entirely to producing a work of art. Perhaps it is even essential. This is clearly a deviant pattern in our age, but we might keep in mind that this was not always so: the young artist's value system duplicates quite closely the prescription for the "good life" outlined by Aristotle.

Turning to the broader personality characteristics of the artist, does rejection of social values mean that artists are not interested in other people? That they are perhaps even actively cold and unfriendly? There is some support for this interpretation. We have evidence that they tend to be withdrawn and cool in their social contacts. They are serious and introspective rather than exuberant and outgoing. Self-sufficiency and the habit of making their own decisions without seeking or relying upon the advice of others round out the characteristic pattern of social withdrawal.

All this suggests that artists dislike other people. But our impression after talking with these students at some length, is that this is simply not the case. They are not misanthropes. They do not reject other people; they reject a social pattern—the casual, self-selling gregariousness accepted as normal behavior by the larger society.

We emerge, then, with a personality profile of the artist as self-sufficient, introspective, and socially withdrawn by the prevailing standards of American society. But how much does this really have to do with creativity? Is there any justification for saying that these are characteristics of a creative personality? The same personality test given to the artists had been administered in another study to 300 eminent scientists—researchers in physics, psychology and biology—and the composite profile obtained bore a striking resemblance to that of the young artists. This strong similarity in personality structure among persons working in such vastly different fields is suggestive, since they are linked only by the element of creative achievement.

Again, it has long been debated whether creativity is related to intelligence. Our art students, when given various IQ type tests, turned out to be no more or less bright than college students. Thus the widespread differences between artists and other students with respect to values and personality were conspicuously lacking in the area of intelligence. It seems, then, that superior IQ may not be essential in art in the way that it is in certain other creative disciplines. We can imagine a man or woman being a highly successful artist without possessing spectacular intellectual powers as indicated by a very high IQ; but it is difficult to imagine a Nobel-prize-winning physicist not having such intellectual powers. It appears that creativity and intelligence may represent different processes and that intelligence is required in widely different degrees in different fields of creative endeavor.

Thus, we began to have some elements of the young artists' profile. We knew the ways in which they were different from "other" people—in their values and personalities—and we knew the many other ways in which they were more nearly similar, notably in intelligence. But all this still told us nothing about what actually happened when they were engaging in the act of artistic creation. What was the process itself like? We decided to find out by watching.

We arranged to have 31 male fine arts students prepare a drawing under realistic studio conditions. We furnished a number of objects to be drawn; the artist could select as many or as few as he wanted and arrange them according to his own preference before beginning to draw. A detailed account of the artist's behavior was kept, both before he began to draw and while he was actually working at the easel. After the drawing was completed, a prolonged interview was held to reconstruct as closely as possible, the conscious mental process of which the artist had been aware while engaged in the experiment. Of the great amount of information collected by these methods, we want to focus here on three very simple points observed for each artist before he began to draw:

☐ the number of objects picked up and examined;

☐ the extent to which he either chose to draw the same objects that everyone else did, or chose more unusual ones;

☐ the extent to which he explored the objects by stroking, weighing, moving their parts, etc.

Now, what was all this supposed to show? We were, of course, looking for something in particular. Our point of view was to conceive of creativity as a special kind of problem-solving process. Problems can be classified according to answers to the following six questions: Has the problem ever been formulated before by the problem-solver? By anyone else? Is the correct method of solution known to the problem-solver? To anyone else? Is the correct solution itself known to the problem-solver? To anyone else? There are certain problems for which the answer is "no" to all six questions. That is, they have never been formulated before, and, once formulated, there is no available method for their solution, nor is there a single correct answer to be reached. It is the formulation and solution of these problems that requires creativity. Actually, these are only potential problems, since they do not exist as problems until someone formulates them as such. Thus, in the case of this special sort of problem, the central question becomes "How are new problems discovered?" rather than the more usual question "How are existing problems solved?" The first step in creative activity involves the discovery, or formulation, of the problem itself.

Returning to our drawing experiment, we can now see why the artist's pre-drawing behavior was important. In picking up, manipulating, exploring and rearranging the objects to be drawn, the artist was trying to formulate an artistic problem. He might pose a problem in form by exploring how the intricate convolutions of a carburetor are related to the equally intricate rhythms of a bunch of grapes. He might formulate a problem of texture by placing a smooth steel shaft next to a battered baseball glove; or he might pose a problem of color—for example, how to give a relatively mono-chromatic drawing color variation—by choosing all his objects in a limited yellow-brown color range. Or he might formulate a problem of spatial relationship by rearranging several objects with little textural or color interest—say, three optical lenses in an unusual, apparently unbalanced or asymmetrical pattern. More likely, his problem would be a complex one, involving some combination of these basic elements of form, texture, color and spatial relationship. And of course the drawings were problematic on a meta-visual dimension as well. One artist, for instance, drew a solitary white sphere in one corner of the paper, and a congeries of other objects in the opposite corner. In the interview he disclosed that on one level the drawing tried to resolve the feeling of loneliness when confronted with a group of people.

As the artist drew, photographs were quietly taken of the drawing as it developed on the paper. The students were not required to stick to the problem as originally formulated; they were allowed to alter or rearrange the objects as they went along, or ignore the objects altogether if, after the beginning, a more interesting problem developed within the confines of the drawing itself. The only requirement we placed on the drawings was that they should satisfy the students' own standards. The completed drawings were then reviewed by a group of established, well-known painters; this panel of experts judged the students' work to be generally of high professional quality.

Now to relate creativity to the drawing process. If creativity lies in the artist's ability to discover and formulate a fresh problem, then his behavior in manipulating, exploring and selecting the elements of his problem—in this case, the objects to be drawn—should have been closely related to the creativity displayed in his finished drawing. This we found to be true. The drawings rated most original and artistically most valuable by the panel of established painters were the ones produced by students who had handled the most objects, explored the objects they handled most closely, and selected the most unusual objects to work with during the pre-drawing, problem-formulating period. These students were not necessarily the ones with the greatest technical skill or "craftsmanship" as rated by the same judges. Here, in what we have labelled "discovery-oriented behavior," seemed to lie a key to the creative process. We interpreted this and similar behavior observed during the execution of the drawing itself as the outward manifestations of a specific cognitive attitude, "concern for discovery." The meaning we inferred from our observations was supported by the interview statements, which revealed that the artist himself was consciously pursuing discovery as opposed to, for instance, expression of feeling or reproduction of beauty alone. This concern with discovery set apart those who were interested in formulating and solving new artistic problems from those who were content merely to apply their technical skill to familiar problems capable of more or less pat solutions.

The most skillful drawings, then, were not always the

Table 1

Correlations Between Discovery Process Variables at the Stage of Problem Formulation and Evaluation of the Artistic Products by Five Artist-Critics (N = 31)

Process Variables	Dimensions of Evaluation		
	Over-all Aesthetic Value (Total 5 Raters)	Originality (Total 5 Raters)	Craftsmanship (Total 5 Raters)
Problem Formulation			
A. Number of objects examined	.48d	.52d	.16
B. Unusualness of objects chosen	.35a	.42c	.22
C. Exploration of objects	.44c	.58e	.34a
Total (ABC)	.40b	.54d	.28

Level of significance = a p<.05
b p<.025
c p<.01
d p<.005
e p<.0005

most original. We are all familiar with this distinction. Contemporary painters have stressed the idea that technical skill without a fresh approach, a new vision, is tedious and dead. Both originality and technical skill are desirable, but without the former there is no progress, there can be no change, whether in the field of art, or of science and technology.

By directly observing the artists' exploratory actions as they worked out new relationships between the problematic elements of their drawings, we learned that such activities may be quite reliable predictors of the creativity displayed in the finished product. And as usual, a research finding poses a further question: Is this process of measurable discovery also involved in the wider range of human creativity, in the more memorable "fruits of originality"?

September/October 1966

FURTHER READING
Daedalus, "Creativity and Learning" Volume 94, No. 3, Summer 1965
The Art of Creation, Arthur Koestler, The Macmillan Company, New York, 1964
Scientific Creativity: Its Recognition and Development, Calvin W. Taylor and Frank Barron, John Wiley and Sons, New York, 1963

THE DEVELOPMENT
AND
UTILIZATION
OF COMPETENCE

Part IV.

A Revolution in Treatment
of the Retarded

GEORGE W. ALBEE

Nearly 6,000,000 Americans are mentally handicapped. By 1970, the number will reach almost 6,500,000. A retarded child is born every four minutes; 126,000 will be born this year.

Largely because of the deep personal interest of President Kennedy, in recent years there has been considerable activity to help the retarded. Since 1963, Federal funds for research and training have increased at an unprecedented rate. Unfortunately, most of these funds are not being used to help the majority of the retarded—those who are normally slow, not victims of inherited or acquired diseases. Instead, money is being poured into costly biomedical research centers and "treatment" clinics to help a minority—those who are retarded because of organic reasons, like injuries, trauma, infections and biochemical imbalances.

The majority of the retarded need, not medical

treatment, but rehabilitative training—so they can use their maximum potential. While every promising research lead should be pursued, and every significant effort in the whole field of retardation should be supported, a truly generous part of the new federal funds ought to be invested in research aimed at helping the retarded lead lives as normal as possible. And more funds should be spent to train people who will, in turn, help train the majority of the retarded.

At the root of this error in priorities is a tragic misconception—namely, that mental retardation is an inherited or acquired disease. Recently, for example, the National Institute of Child Health and Human Development announced that it was allocating new funds for research centers whose purpose will be to 1) discover organic causes of retardation and 2) mount medical efforts to reduce its incidence. The Institute's press release went on: "Inherited diseases are among the leading causes of mental retardation." On May 16, 1967, the U.S. Public Health Service announced a grant for the construction of a $2.2 million center for medical research at a Midwestern university. Its press release stated:

> Several research studies will be aimed at identifying metabolic abnormalities in patients with unknown causes of mental retardation. Through biochemical studies of the urine, blood, and tissues of retarded patients, defects or absences of necessary biologic metabolic enzymes may be uncovered, paving the way for new attacks on mental retardation.

Between the lines of both statements is the promise that the incidence of retardation, because of such medically oriented research, may be significantly reduced. This promise is based on ignorance—or on a distortion of reality.

The truth is that most retardation is *not* an inherited disease. Quite correctly, President Kennedy's Panel on Mental Retardation emphasized the fact that

> ... about 75 percent to 85 percent of those now diagnosed as retarded show no demonstrable gross brain abnormality. They are, by and large, persons with relatively mild degrees of retardation . . . . Unfavorable environmental and psychological influences are thought to play an important contributory role among this group. Such influences include interference with normal emotional and intellectual stimulation in early infancy, unfavorable psychological or emotional experiences in early childhood, and lack of normal intellectual and cultural experiences during the entire developmental period.

More basically, brightness and dullness are a reflection of inherited capacities—the result of the interaction of a large number of genes operating in a perfectly normal, nonpathological way. While intelligence is thus genetically determined, so is a person's height—and neither stature *nor* mental retardation is an illness.

People are born retarded simply because intelligence is distributed normally throughout the entire population. A certain percentage of all children—slightly more than 2 percent, as it happens—will be born without defect and yet have I.Q.s below 70. Similarly, a certain percentage—also 2 percent—will be born with an I.Q. as high as that of the average graduate student.

Edward Zigler of Yale put it this way:

> We need simply to accept the generally recognized

fact that the gene pool of any population is such that there will always be variations in the behavioral . . . expression of virtually every measurable trait or characteristic of man. From the polygenic model advanced by geneticists, we deduce that the distribution of intelligence is characterized by a bisymmetrical bell-shaped curve . . . .

Once one adopts the position that the familial mental retardate is not defective or pathological but is essentially a normal individual of low intelligence, then the familial retardate no longer represents a mystery but, rather, is viewed as a particular manifestation of the general developmental process.

This point has crucial implications. It illuminates the inappropriateness of our present priorities, whereby 90 to 95 percent of the federal construction funds for retardation centers will be used to house research and training on biomedical approaches. It says the large majority of retarded children and adults are *not* retarded because of an acquired physiological abnormality, or because of a defect in their metabolism, or because of brain injury, or because their mothers had German measles, or because of the effects of any other infectious disease, or because of any other discovered or undiscovered exogenous or biomedical defects.

Rather, the majority of retarded children and adults are produced from the more or less accidental distribution of polygenic factors present in the entire human race. Each parent transmits—often untouched—a large and varied set of genetic potentials from his myriad ancestors to his descendants. Thus each human is potentially the parent or grandparent or greatgrandparent of a retarded child. Because of various forms of gene linkage, "familial" retardation is somewhat less common in bright families than in dull families. It occurs most commonly in "average" families—because there are many more of them.

The cold, but realistic, fact must be faced: It is no more likely that medical research findings will raise the intelligence of most retardates than it is that research will raise the intelligence of college students.

Let me make it very clear that I am not opposing medical research, or deprecating the triumphs of biology and medicine in uncovering the causes of several (albeit rare) forms of retardation in the past decade or so. What I am arguing against is the almost exclusive investment of federal monies in medically-oriented research. For the plain truth is that, even after all the post-conception organic causes and all the metabolic and chromosomal defects are discovered and prevented or corrected, at least 2 percent of the general population will *still* be born retarded. And this situation will prevail for the indefinite future.

I believe, therefore, that it is not only unfair but unreasonable that almost every new federally funded, university-affiliated center to train people and to engage in research in this field is in a medically-dominated and biomedically-oriented center. Even in the Mental Retardation Research Centers being funded by the new National Institute of Child Health and Human Development, the major efforts are biomedical. Instead, at least half of these centers should be designed for research in special educational methods and rehabilitation; others should be designed primarily for research in the social and behavioral-science approaches to helping the retarded.

Why is the emphasis, both in research and in treatment, on organic approaches to retardation? One reason: the academic medical institutions' insatiable need for research money. Because of the enormous federal funds recently made available for constructing research and training facilities in the area of retardation, medicine—particularly psychiatry and pediatrics—has discovered and promulgated compelling arguments why these research centers should be placed in medical settings. Almost exclusive emphasis has been on all of the external causes of retardation—the metabolic, the infectious, the undiscovered causes of brain damage. In addition, by controlling the advisory committees that rule on applications for construction funds to build the university-affiliated facilities, the doctors have controlled the character of these centers still further.

Another reason: The powerful citizens' committees in the field of retardation are composed largely of well-informed parents of retarded children. But in these families, normal garden-variety retardation is relatively rare. These parents, from the numerically small but politically advantaged upper-middle classes and upper classes, are more likely to have children who are retarded because of *exogenous* damage than because of normal polygenic inheritance. Their retarded children are more likely to be represented in the below-50 I.Q. group of the seriously-handicapped than among the much more common 50-70 I.Q. group. As a consequence, these citizens' committees militate for biomedical discoveries that will prevent, or cure, exogenous retardation. Their aspirations coincide with the eagerness of academic medicine to have large, expensive research labs. Both groups push legislation—and the rules implementing legislation—in the direction of an overwhelming emphasis on biomedical research.

There are still other reasons to explain the over-emphasis on biological or injury explanations of retardation.

In child-worshipping American society, and particularly in the great sprawling suburban areas, parents are gravely concerned about the academic success of their children. Their children's scores on intelligence tests are therefore exceedingly important to these parents. And when a parent is told that his child tests at the 135-I.Q. level, his response is a feeling of pride, even elation. It means that Johnny can go far, that a society that rewards intellectual success (not necessarily achievement) will eventually be at his feet.

But consider the parent who is told that his child is functioning at a 65-I.Q. level and must be placed in a special class for slow-learners. After his original shock and panic have subsided somewhat, the parent begins to cast about for an explanation. What could have happened? What accident, injury or disease could have caused this terrible thing?

Now, two currently popular diagnoses for mentally deficient children are *minimal brain damage,* or *maturational lag.* The trouble is that the neurological and psychological tests upon which these diagnoses are based leave much to be desired. Nevertheless, one or the other of these diagnoses is made with increasing frequency, perhaps because they are very useful to give to parents who somehow feel personally responsible for a retarded child and seize upon such a diagnosis as an exculpation.

It is difficult for a pediatrician, a psychiatrist or a consulting psychologist to tell parents their child is just slow mentally, and not because of illness, disease or exogenous damage. Similarly, one of the most difficult diagnoses for parents in our society to accept is that their child is normal and has a limited intellectual capacity. No special explanation is required for a child who is bright—he "just comes by that naturally." But when a child is slow intellectually, something must have happened. Thus the diagnosis of minimal brain damage, or maturational lag, has great psychological appeal. Most parents can recall an illness or accident at some point in the child's life, or in the expectant mother's. This is certainly an easier explanation to accept, in an extremely painful situation, than garden-variety, normal retardation. Nor is it hard to understand that such a parent's desire to "do something" leads to still more support of biomedical research.

Whatever the reasons for its origin, the imbalance in the field of mental retardation should be remedied swiftly—if our society truly believes that everyone should have the opportunity to develop his potential to the maximum. We need social and educational research into retardation as much—or more—than we need biological and medical research. What follows is just one example of a recent significant study involving teachers, children and intelligence (Robert Rosenthal and Lenore Jacobsen, 1967).

At the beginning of the school year, intelligence tests were given to children in a city school of 18 classrooms (three at each grade level from first to sixth). By pre-arranged plan, the teachers in the school were told that the tests measured potential for "intellectual blooming." One child in five—chosen at random—in each classroom was said to have scored high on the test. This child, the teacher was told, very probably would show marked intellectual improvement within the next several months.

Eight months later, at the end of the school year,

another intelligence test was given. The specially-identified children in the first and second grades had made dramatic improvements. In first grade, the average gain was more than 15 points; in the second grade, more than ten points. In actuality, these children had been randomly chosen for identification. Yet, by some mysterious alchemy, the teachers had behaved in such a way toward these young children, who were designated as special, as to elicit more of their basic potential.

This study illustrates how research can clarify a point that is of crucial importance in planning educational experiences for intellectually handicapped youngsters. The point made in the study is that teachers with the right attitudes and expectations are of critical importance—and can have a significant effect on the development of the child's capacity to its fullest. This is the sort of research we need more of!

Too often we approach the task of teaching retarded children with the expectation that they will not, or cannot, learn. We have not yet begun to tap much of the potential of these children, a potential that might be unlocked not only with new techniques but with new expectations. Such insights and progress, of course, will *not* result from our exclusive reliance on biological research.

But it is not only research efforts that are out of balance. So are efforts at rehabilitation.

For example, the Children's Bureau of the Department of Health, Education and Welfare has struggled painfully—for 11 years—to develop 134 clinics across the nation for the retarded. These clinics ostensibly are operated to demonstrate the value of biomedically-oriented treatment that uses a so-called multi-disciplinary approach. As J. William Oberman (technical adviser on Medical Aspects of Mental Retardation for the Children's Bureau) notes somewhat plaintively, these 134 clinics are able to offer only a very small fraction of the amount of care needed by the retarded and their families. He estimates that each year some 30,000 individuals are served by these clinics and that perhaps "other multidisciplinary clinics under medical direction" provide care for an additional 10,000 retarded children. But this is a trifle compared with the needs of the 6 million retarded children and adults in the United States. Dr. Oberman notes that even 2,500 new clinics (as impossible to staff as 2,500 new major-league baseball teams!) could barely handle the present demand. And the demand keeps increasing. Unmet needs grow. Of what profit is it to demonstrate that an expensive treatment clinic, expertly staffed with high-priced professionals, can see a handful of children a year with modest effectiveness, when it is impossible ever to duplicate such clinics? How long will Congress stand still for this nonsense?

The justification for these clinics having medical direction and treatment (largely unavailable full-time) rests on two highly emotional arguments. One, as we have seen, stresses the pathological or accidental—and theoretically preventable—causes of a high percentage of the severely retarded. The second stresses the concomitant additional physical handicaps, which are alleged to require continuing diagnostic follow-up and medical care.

The truth is that 85 percent of the retarded, after thorough medical evaluation, ordinarily require no more medical care than many other handicapped groups in society. The associated physical complications that are correctable, in a majority of cases, are visual and auditory—outside the competence of the ordinary psychiatrist or pediatrician. A significant number of retardates also have speech problems, and these demand the special skills of a speech therapist rather than a physician.

The kind of professional manpower required for effective and functional care of the retarded is not more physicians, nurses and psychologists with highly specialized training in this field. These people do not spend any significant amount of their professional time working with the retarded anyway. More than anything else, we need teachers and vocational-guidance specialists.

According to the President's Panel, a very large majority of the retarded "can, with special training and assistance, acquire limited job skills and achieve a high measure of independence; they represent 85 percent of the retarded group." Yet many states even now do not provide any classes for the "trainable" retarded, and no state has enough classes for the "educable" retarded. Only one of every five retarded children is now being reached by any kind of special-education program. The President's Panel found 20,000 special-education teachers across the nation, many of them poorly trained, where 55,000 were needed. The panel predicted that by 1970 the need for special teachers will reach 90,000. And state vocational agencies that provide urgently-needed vocational rehabilitation for the mildly retarded are currently reaching only 3 percent of them.

In one investigation in Massachusetts, Simon Olshansky studied over 1,000 children whose families were receiving aid for dependent children. He found that 6.7 percent were retarded. Virtually none were getting any significant help. The mothers were "too immobilized" to recognize the problem, or to seek help. Social agencies, as is frequently the case, had no workers to reach out and seek cases that would add to their excessive caseloads.

To provide adequate help to the 110,000 children born each year with mild but handicapping retardation, and to provide care and rehabilitation for the other 5,500,000 mildly retarded people in our society, we need teachers, teachers and more teachers—and then taxes to support a massive educational effort. Among teachers in this context I include all those specially trained and devoted professional people willing to spend hours and hours in daily and patient interaction with retarded children, unlocking and strengthening whatever skills and abilities are in them. Also included are the vocational-rehabilitation workers and those in occupational therapy, in recreational therapy and in non-professional but patient and warm interaction therapies that the retarded yearn for.

Needed desperately, in addition to teachers, are skilled caseworkers, sheltered-workshop personnel, vocational-guidance counselors, speech therapists, and all of the range of other people who have chosen careers that make them their handicapped brother's keeper. Many of these people could be trained in bachelor's or even two-year junior-college programs.

But, first and foremost, it is essential to escape the biomedical orientation that controls our efforts. Fourteen university-affiliated facilities for the retarded, all devoted to research and training, have now been approved for construction with federal funds. The federal government already has allocated the millions of dollars to build these research centers. Every last one of them is in a medical setting where most of the research, the research training, and the education of professionals will be relevant to a small minority of retarded children. What have these huge new research centers to do with training special-education teachers and vocational counselors? The answer: next to nothing.

There *is* a place where medical care is truly needed to prevent retardation, and where it has not been available—in the prenatal and perinatal care of "medically indigent" expectant mothers in our large cities. A significant number of their children are born prematurely, and the prematurity rate is two to three times greater in low-income families where prenatal care is haphazard. Almost 500,000 indigent mothers deliver babies each year in our tax-supported city hospitals. At least 100,000 of these need special medical services for complications in pregnancy and birth. Most of them do not get it.

Here is an area for good medical research and action, because mental retardation that may well have an organic base is associated with prematurity and low birth weight. Among infants who weigh below three pounds at birth, nearly three-quarters subsequently develop physical or mental defects. In an average big-city hospital, the baby girl born to a Negro mother on the "staff service" (free service) weighs nearly a pound less than the baby born to a suburban white mother on the private service of the general hospital. A large percentage of urban indigent Negro mothers are "walk-ins" who receive little or no prenatal care, no special instructions on diet, and no medical guidance until labor pains begin. The retardation rate in infants born to these indigent mothers is ten times the white rate.

If American medicine were to turn its massive

resources to the solution of these problems—adequate medical care for the poor—many more cases of retardation could be prevented than will result from the present emphasis on research into esoteric causes. Unfortunately, the growing shortage of physicians, the fee-for-service philosophy of American medicine, and the high prestige of complex research activities in academia all combine to make this significant prevention-effort unlikely.

At the root of our double standard of care and intervention with the retarded is the fact that the nice people—the people who do the planning, the governing, the writing, the reading and the decision-making in our society—are members of the economically favored group. Most of them have arranged their lives in such a way as to be sealed off—geographically and socially—from the have-not groups, the disadvantaged and the dispossessed.

But parents of the retarded—parent-citizen groups in particular—are, for the most part, prosperous, and they at least have the advantage of some special insights into some of the darker social forces in our society. Most of them know from personal experience the hardships and heartaches that are the lot of the child or adult in our society who has limited intellectual capacity. Such citizen groups must take the lead in demanding that at least half of the tax dollars be spent for educational and rehabilitative approaches for all our intellectually-handicapped children and adults.

Our efforts are out of balance and out of joint. It is only an informed citizenry that can study the facts and act on them. The retarded cannot speak for themselves.

January/February 1968

FURTHER READING:

A Proposed Program for National Action to Combat Mental Retardation (U.S. Public Health Service, 1962). Report of the President's Panel on Mental Retardation. A good overview of the problem and of the recommendations to President Kennedy.

Intelligence and Experience by J. McV. Hunt (New York: The Ronald Press, 1961). While somewhat technical and research-oriented, this is an excellent treatise on factors influencing intelligent behavior.

The Wild Boy of Aveyron by J.M.G. Itard (New York: Appleton-Century-Crofts, 1932). This report of the attempt of a nine-teenth-century physician to teach a mentally retarded boy is a classic.

Psychopathology of Childhood by Jane W. Kessler (Englewood Cliffs, N.J.: Prentice-Hall, 1966). This excellent textbook has chapters summarizing historical and contemporary approaches to mental subnormality and to learning problems.

Early Education of the Mentally Retarded by S. Kirk (Urbana, Ill.: University of Illinois Press, 1958). All of Dr. Kirk's writings must be on any required-reading list in this field.

Psychological Problems in Mental Deficiency (Third Edition) by S. Sarason (New York: Harper & Row, 1958). Dr. Sarason has pioneered in the development of a psychoeducational clinic at Yale that is a model for a meaningful approach to the problem discussed in this article.

Changing the Game from "Get the Teacher" to "Learn"

ROBERT L. HAMBLIN, DAVID BUCKHOLDT
DONALD BUSHELL, DESMOND ELLIS
and DANIEL FERRITOR

Almost any educator of experience will assure you that it is next to impossible—and often actually impossible—to teach normal classroom subjects to children who have extreme behavior problems, or who are "too young." Yet at four experimental classrooms of the Central Midwestern Regional Educational Laboratories (CEMREL), we have been bringing about striking changes in the behavior and learning progress of just such children.

In the 18 months of using new exchange systems and working with different types of problem children, we have seen these results:

☐ Extraordinarily aggressive boys, who had not previously responded to therapy, have been tamed.

☐ Two-year-olds have learned to read about as fast and as well as their five-year-old classmates.

☐ Four ghetto children, too shy, too withdrawn to talk,

210

have become better than average talkers.

□ Several autistic children, who were either mute or could only parrot sounds, have developed functional speech, have lost their bizarre and disruptive behavior patterns, and their relationships with parents and other children have improved. All of these children are on the road to normality.

Our system is deceptively simple. Superficially, in fact, it may not even seem new—though, in detail, it has never been tried in precisely this form in the classroom before. In essence, we simply reinforce "good" behavior and nonpunitively discourage "bad" behavior. We structure a social exchange so that as the child progresses, we reinforce this behavior—give him something that he values, something that shows our approval. Therefore, he becomes strongly motivated to continue his progress. To terminate bizarre, disruptive or explosive patterns, we stop whatever has been reinforcing that undesirable behavior—actions or attention that teachers or parents have unwittingly been giving him in exchange, often in the belief that they were punishing and thus discouraging him. Study after study has shown that whenever a child persists in behaving badly, some adult has, perhaps inadvertently, been rewarding him for it.

"Socialization" is the term that sociologists use to describe the process of transforming babies—who can do little but cry, eat and sleep—into adults who can communicate and function rather effectively in their society. Socialization varies from culture to culture, and while it is going on all around us, we are seldom aware of it. But when normal socialization breaks down, "problems" occur—autism, nonverbal or hyperaggressive behavior, retardation, delinquency, crime and so on.

The authors, after years of often interesting but by

and large frustrating research, realized that the more common theories of child development (Freudian, neo-Freudian, the developmental theories of Gesell and Piaget, and a number of others) simply do not satisfactorily explain the socialization process in children. Consequently in desperation we began to move toward the learning theories and then toward the related exchange theories of social structure. Since then, working with problem children, our view has gradually been amplified and refined. Each experimental classroom has given us a different looking glass. In each we can see the child in different conditions, and can alter the conditions which hinder his socialization into a civilized, productive adult capable of happiness.

By the time they become students, most children love to play with one another, to do art work, to cut and paste, to play with Playdoh, to climb and swing on the playground, and so on. Most pre-schools also serve juice and cookie snacks, and some have television sets or movies. There is, consequently, no dearth of prizes for us to reward the children for good behavior. The problem is not in finding reinforcers, but in managing them.

One of the simpler and most effective ways, we found, was to develop a token-exchange system. The tokens we use are plastic discs that children can earn. A child who completes his arithmetic or reading may earn a dozen tokens, given one by one as he proceeds through the lessons. And at the end of the lesson period comes the reward.

Often it is a movie. The price varies. For four tokens, a student can watch while sitting on the floor; for eight, he gets a chair; for 12, he can watch while sitting on the table. Perhaps the view is better from the table—

anyway, the children almost always buy it if they have enough tokens. But if they dawdled so much that they earned fewer than four, they are "timed out" into the hall while the others see the movie. Throughout the morning, therefore, the children earn, then spend, then earn, then spend.

This token-exchange system is very powerful. It can create beneficial changes in a child's behavior, his emotional reactions and ultimately even his approach to life. But it is not easy to set up, nor simple to maintain.

At the beginning the tokens are meaningless to the children; so to make them meaningful, we pair them with M&M candies, or something similar. As the child engages in the desired behavior (or a reasonable facsimile), the teacher gives him a "Thank you," an M&M and a token. At first the children are motivated by the M&Ms and have to be urged to hold on to the tokens; but then they find that the tokens can be used to buy admission to the movie, Playdoh or other good things. The teacher tells them the price and asks them to count out the tokens. Increasingly, the teacher "forgets" the M&Ms. In two or three days the children get no candy, just the approval and the tokens. By then, they have learned.

There are problems in maintaining a token exchange. Children become disinterested in certain reinforcers if they are used too frequently, and therefore in the tokens that buy them. For instance, young children will work very hard to save up tokens to play with Playdoh once a week; if they are offered Playdoh every day, the charm quickly fades. Some activities—snacks, movies, walks outdoors—are powerful enough to be used every day.

As noted, the children we worked with had different

behavior problems, reflecting various kinds of breakdowns in the socialization process. Each experiment we
conducted concentrated on a particular type of malad-
justment or a particular group of maladjusted children
to see how a properly structured exchange system might
help them. Let us look at each experiment, to see how
each problem was affected.

Unfortunately, our world reinforces and rewards
aggressive behavior. Some cultures and some families are
open and brazen about it—they systematically and
consciously teach their young that it is desirable, and
even virtuous, to attack certain other individuals or
groups. The child who can beat up the other kids on the
playground is sometimes respected by his peers, and
perhaps by his parents; the soldier achieves glory in
combat. The status, the booty or the bargaining
advantages that come to the aggressor can become
reinforcement to continue and escalate his aggressions.

In more civilized cultures the young are taught not to
use aggression, and we try to substitute less harmful
patterns. But even so, aggression is sometimes reinforced
unintentionally—and the consequences, predictably, are
the same as if the teaching was deliberate.

In the long run civilized cultures are not kind to
hyperaggressive children. A recent survey in England,
for instance, found that the great majority of teachers
felt that aggressive behavior by students disturbed more
classrooms than anything else and caused the most
anxiety among teachers. At least partly as a result, the
dropout rates for the hyperaggressives was two and
one-half times as great as for "normals," and disproportionate numbers of hyperaggressives turned up in mental
clinics.

The traditional treatment for aggressive juveniles is

punishment—often harsh punishment. This is not only of dubious moral value, but generally it does not work.

We took seriously—perhaps for the first time—the theory that aggression is a type of exchange behavior. Boys become aggressive because they get something for it; they continue to be aggressive because the rewards are continuing. To change an aggressive pattern in our experimental class at Washington University, therefore, we had to restructure appropriately the exchange system in which the boys were involved.

As subjects we (Ellis and Hamblin) found five extraordinarily aggressive four-year-old boys, all referred to us by local psychiatrists and social workers who had been able to do very little with them. Next, we hired a trained teacher. We told her about the boys and general nature of the experiment—then gave her her head. That is, she was allowed to use her previous training during the first period—and this would provide a baseline comparison with that followed after. We hoped she would act like the "typical teacher." We suspect that she did.

The teacher was, variously, a strict disciplinarian, wise counselor, clever arbitrator and sweet peacemaker. Each role failed miserably. After the eighth day, the average of the children was 150 sequences of aggression per day! Here is what a mere four minutes of those sequences were like:

Mike, John and Dan are seated together playing with pieces of Playdoh. Barry, some distance from the others, is seated and also is playing with Playdoh. The children, except Barry, are talking about what they are making. Time is 9:10 AM. Miss Sally, the teacher, turns toward the children and says, "It's time for a lesson. Put your Playdoh away." Mike says,

"Not me." John says, "Not me." Dan says, "Not
me." Miss Sally moves toward Mike. Mike throws
some Playdoh in Miss Sally's face. Miss Sally jerks
back, then moves forward rapidly and snatches
Playdoh from Mike. Puts Playdoh in her pocket. Mike
screams for Playdoh, says he wants to play with it.
Mike moves toward Miss Sally and attempts to snatch
the Playdoh from Miss Sally's pocket. Miss Sally
pushes him away. Mike kicks Miss Sally on the leg.
Kicks her again, and demands the return of his
Playdoh. Kicks Miss Sally again. Picks up a small steel
chair and throws it at Miss Sally. Miss Sally jumps out
of the way. Mike picks up another chair and throws it
more violently. Miss Sally cannot move in time. Chair
strikes her foot. Miss Sally pushes Mike down on the
floor. Mike starts up. Pulls over one chair. Now
another, another. Stops a moment. Miss Sally is
picking up chairs, Mike looks at Miss Sally. Miss
Sally moves toward Mike. Mike runs away.

John wants his Playdoh. Miss Sally says "No." He
joins Mike in pulling over chairs and attempts to grab
Playdoh from Miss Sally's pocket. Miss Sally pushes
him away roughly. John is screaming that he wants to
play with his Playdoh. Moves toward phonograph.
Pulls it off the table; lets it crash onto the floor. Mike
has his coat on. Says he is going home. Miss Sally asks
Dan to bolt the door. Dan gets to the door at the
same time as Mike. Mike hits Dan in the face. Dan's
nose is bleeding. Miss Sally walks over to Dan, turns
to the others, and says that she is taking Dan to the
washroom and that while she is away, they may play
with the Playdoh. Returns Playdoh from pocket to
Mike and John. Time: 9:14 AM.

Wild? Very. These were barbarous little boys who

enjoyed battle. Miss Sally did her best but they were just more clever than she, and they *always* won. Whether Miss Sally wanted to or not, they could always drag her into the fray, and just go at it harder and harder until she capitulated. She was finally driven to their level, trading a kick for a kick and a spit in the face for a spit in the face.

What Miss Sally did not realize is that she had inadvertently structured an exchange where she consistently reinforced aggression. First, as noted, whenever she fought with them, she *always lost*. Second, more subtly, she reinforced their aggressive pattern by giving it serious attention—by looking, talking, scolding, cajoling, becoming angry, even striking back. These boys were playing a teasing game called "Get the Teacher." The more she showed that she was bothered by their behavior, the better they liked it, and the further they went.

These interpretations may seem far-fetched, but they are borne out dramatically by what happened later. On the twelfth day we changed the conditions, beginning with B1 (see Figure 1). First, we set up the usual token exchange to reinforce cooperative behavior. This was to develop or strengthen behavior that would replace aggression. Any strong pattern of behavior serves some function for the individual, so the first step in getting rid of a strong, disruptive pattern is substituting another one that is more useful and causes fewer problems. Not only therapy, but simple humanity dictates this.

First, the teacher had to be instructed in how *not* to reinforce aggression. Contrary to all her experience, she was asked to turn her back on the aggressor, and at the same time to reinforce others' cooperation with tokens. Once we were able to coach her and give her immediate feedback over a wireless-communication system, she structured the exchanges almost perfectly. The data in Figures 1 and 2 show the crucial changes: a gradual increase in cooperation—from 56 to about 115 sequences per day, and a corresponding decrease in aggression from 150 to about 60 sequences!

These results should have been satisfactory, but we were new at this kind of experimentation, and nervous. We wanted to reduce the frequency of aggression to a "normal" level, to about 15 sequences a day. So we restructured the exchange system and thus launched A2.

In A2, we simply made sure that aggression would

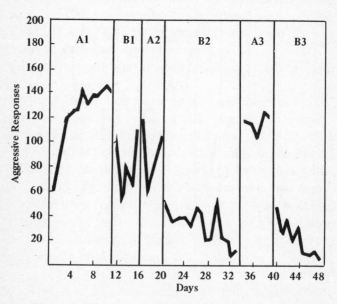

Figure 1. Frequency of aggressive sequences by days for five 4-year-old boys. In A1, A2 and A3 the teacher attempted to punish aggression but inadvertently reinforced it. In B1, B2 and B3 she turned her back or otherwise ignored aggression and thus did not reinforce it.

always be punished. The teacher was told to *charge* tokens for any aggression.

To our surprise, the frequency of cooperation remained stable, about 115 sequences per day; but aggression *increased* to about 110 sequences per day! Evidently the boys were still playing "Get the Teacher," and the fines were enough reinforcement to increase aggression.

So, instead of fining the children, the teacher was again told to ignore aggression by turning her back and giving attention and tokens only for cooperation. The

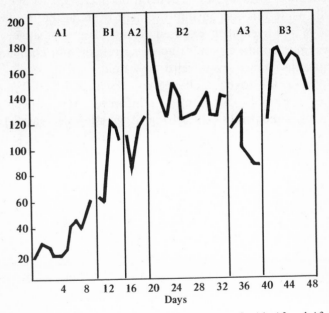

Figure 2. Frequency of cooperative sequences. In A1, A2 and A3 the teacher structured a weak approval exchange for cooperation and a disapproval exchange for noncooperation. In B1, A2, B2 and B3, she structured a token exchange for cooperation.

frequency of aggression went down to a near "normal" level, about 16 sequences per day (B2), and cooperation increased to about 140 sequences.

Then, as originally planned, the conditions were again reversed. The boys were given enough tokens at the beginning of the morning to buy their usual supply of movies, toys and snacks, and these were not used as reinforcers. The teacher was told to do the best she could. She was not instructed to return to her old pattern, but without the tokens and without our coaching she did—and with the same results. Note A3 in Figures 1 and 2. Aggression increased to about 120 sequences per day, and cooperation decreased to about 90. While this was an improvement over A1, before the boys had ever been exposed to the token exchange, it was not good. The mixture of aggression and cooperation was strange, even weird, to watch.

When the token exchange was restructured (B3) and the aggression no longer reinforced, the expected changes recurred—with a bang. Aggression decreased to seven sequences on the last day, and cooperation rose to about 181 sequences. In "normal" nursery schools, our observations have shown that five boys can be expected to have 15 aggression sequences and 60 cooperation sequences per day. Thus, from extremely aggressive and uncooperative, our boys had become less aggressive and far more cooperative than "normal" boys.

Here is an example of their new behavior patterns, taken from a rest period—precisely the time when the most aggressive acts had occurred in the past:

All of the children are sitting around the table drinking their milk; John, as usual, has finished first. Takes his plastic mug and returns it to the table. Miss Martha, the assistant teacher, gives him a token. John goes to the cupboard, takes out his mat, spreads it out by the blackboard, and lies down. Miss Martha gives him a token. Meanwhile, Mike, Barry, and Jack have spread their mats on the carpet. Dan is lying on the carpet itself since he hasn't a mat. Each of them gets a token. Mike asks if he can sleep by the wall. Miss Sally says "Yes." John asks if he can put out the light. Miss Sally says to wait until Barry has his mat spread properly. Dan asks Mike if he can share his mat with him. Mike says "No." Dan then asks Jack. Jack says, "Yes," but before he can move over, Mike says "Yes." Dan joins Mike. Both Jack and Mike get tokens. Mike and Jack get up to put their tokens in their cans. Return to their mats. Miss Sally asks John to put out the light. John does so. Miss Martha gives him a token. All quiet now. Four minutes later—all quiet. Quiet still, three minutes later. Time: 10:23 AM. Rest period ends.

The hyperaggressive boys actually had, and were, double problems; they were not only extremely disruptive, but they were also washouts as students. Before the token system (A1), they paid attention to their teacher only about 8 percent of the lesson time (see Figure 3). The teacher's system of scolding the youngsters for inattention and taking their attention for granted with faint approval, if any, did not work at all. To the pupils, the "Get the Teacher" game was much more satisfying.

After the token exchange was started, in B1, B2, B3 and B4, it took a long, long time before there was any appreciable effect. The teacher was being trained from scratch, and our methods were, then, not very good. However, after we set up a wireless-communication system that allowed us to coach the teacher from behind a one-way mirror and to give her immediate feedback, the children's attention began to increase. Toward the end of B3, it leveled off at about 75 percent—from 8 percent! After the token exchange was taken out during A2, attention went down to level off at 23 percent; put back in at B4, it shot back up to a plateau of about 93 percent. Like a roller coaster: 8 percent without, to 75 with, to 23 without, to 93 with.

These results occurred with chronic, apparently hopeless hyperaggressive boys. Would token exchange also help "normal," relatively bright upper-middle-class children? Sixteen youngsters of that description—nine boys and seven girls, ranging from 2 years 9 months to 4

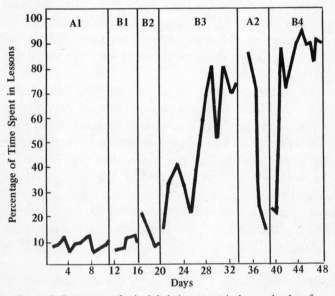

Figure 3. Percentage of scheduled time spent in lessons by days for five hyperaggressive boys. In A1 and A2, teacher structured approval exchange for attendance, disapproval for non-attendance. In B1 and B2, a token exchange for attendance was structured, but not effectively until B2 and B4.

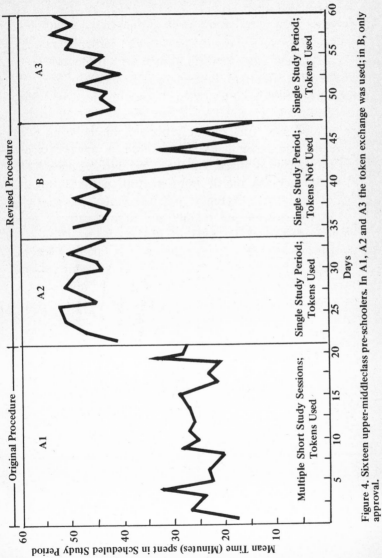

Figure 4. Sixteen upper-middleclass pre-schoolers. In A1, A2 and A3 the token exchange was used; in B, only approval.

years 9 months—were put through an experimental series by Bushell, Hamblin and Denis Stoddard in an experimental pre-school at Webster College. All had about a month's earlier experience with the token-exchange system. The results are shown in Figure 4.

At first, the study hour was broken up into 15-minute periods, alternating between the work that received tokens, and the play or reward that the tokens could be used for. Probably because the children were already familiar with token exchange, no great increase in learning took place. On the 22nd day, we decided to try to increase the learning period, perhaps for the whole hour. In A2 (Figure 4), note that the time spent in studying went up rapidly and dramatically—almost doubling—from 27 to level off at 42 minutes.

During B, the token exchange was taken out completely. The teachers still gave encouragement and prepared interesting lessons as before. The rewards—the nature walks, snacks, movies and so on—were retained. But, as in a usual classroom, they were given to the children free instead of being sold. The children continued at about the same rate as before for a few days. But after a week, attention dropped off slowly, then sharply. On the last day it was down to about 15 minutes—one-third the level of the end of the token period.

In A3, the token exchange was reinstituted. In only three days, attention snapped back from an average of 15 minutes to 45 minutes. However, by the end of A3, the students paid attention an average of 50 of the available 60 minutes.

A comparison of the record of these normals with the record of the hyperaggressive boys is interesting. The increase in attention brought by the token exchange, from about 15 minutes to 50, is approximately three-fold for the normal children; but for the hyperaggressive boys—who are disobedient and easily distracted—it is about eleven-fold, from 8 percent to 93 percent of the time. The increase was not only greater, but the absolute level achieved was higher. This indicates strongly, therefore, that the more problematic the child, the greater may be the effect of token exchange on his behavior.

The high rates of attention were not due to the fact that each teacher had fewer children to work with. Individualized lessons were not enough. Without the token exchange, even three teachers could not hold the interest of 16 children two to four years old—at least not in reading, writing and arithmetic.

Praise and approval were not enough as rewards. The teachers, throughout the experiment, used praise and approval to encourage attention; they patted heads and said things like "Good," "You're doing fine," and "Keep it up"; yet, in B, when the token exchange was removed, this attention nevertheless ultimately declined by two-thirds. Social approval is important, but not nearly so powerful as material reinforcers.

Finally, it is obvious that if the reinforcers (movies, snacks, toys or whatever) do not seem directly connected to the work, they will not sustain a high level of study. To be effective with young children, rewards must occur in a structured exchange in which they are given promptly as recompense and thus are directly connected to the work performed.

According to accepted educational theory, a child must be about six and a half before he can comfortably learn to read. But is this really true, or is it merely a convenience for the traditional educational system?

After all, by the time a normal child is two and a half he has learned a foreign language—the one spoken by his parents and family; and he has learned it without special instruction or coaching. He has even developed a feel for the rules of grammar, which, by and large, he uses correctly. It is a rare college student who becomes fluent in a foreign language with only two and a half years of formal training—and our college students are supposed to be the brightest of our breed. Paul Goodman has suggested that if children learned to *speak* by the same methods that they learn to *read,* there might well be as many nonspeakers now as illiterates.

What if the problem is really one of motivation? If we structured an exchange that rewarded them, in ways they could appreciate, for learning to read, couldn't they learn as readily as five-year-olds?

We decided that for beginners, the number of words a child can read is the best test of reading ability. In an experiment designed by Hamblin, Carol Pfeiffer, Dennis Shea and June Hamblin, and administered at our Washington University pre-school, the token-exchange system was used to reward children for the number of words each learned. The results are given in Figure 5. Note that the two-year-olds did about as well as the five-year-olds; their sight vocabularies were almost as large.

There was an interesting side effect: at the end of the school year, all but one of these children tested at the "genius" level. On Stanford-Binet individual tests, their IQ scores increased as much as 36 points. It was impossible to compute an average gain only because three of the children "topped out"—made something in excess of 149, the maximum score possible.

In general, the lower the measured IQ at the start, the

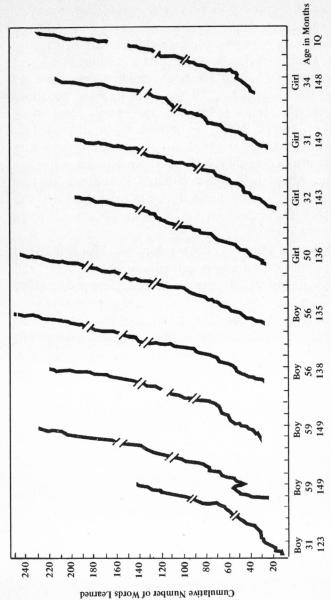

Figure 5. Number of sight-words learned through time by five 4- and 5-year-olds, and four 2- and 3-year-olds. Note that the younger children did about as well as the older ones—except for one boy whose IQ was somewhat lower than the others in the group. (Gaps indicate absences.)

greater the gain—apparently as a result of the educational experience.

What happens when ghetto children are introduced
into a token-exchange system? At our Mullanphy Street
pre-school, 22 Afro-American children—age three to
five—attend regularly. All live in or near the notorious
Pruitt-Igoe Housing Project, and most come from
broken homes. When the school began, the teachers
were unenthusiastic about a token exchange, so we let
them proceed as they wished. The result was pandemo-
nium. About half of the children chased one another
around the room, engaged in violent arguments and
fought. The others withdrew; some would not even
communicate.

After the third day, the teachers asked for help. As in
the other experimental schools, we (Buckholdt and
Hamblin) instructed them to ignore aggressive-disruptive
behavior and to reward attention and cooperation with
social approval and the plastic tokens, later to be
exchanged for such things as milk, cookies, admission to
the movies and toys. The children quickly caught on,
the disruptions diminished, and cooperation increased.
Within three weeks of such consistent treatment, most
of the children took part in the lessons, and disruptive
behavior had become only an occasional problem. All of
this, remember, without punishment.

Our attention was then focused upon the children
with verbal problems. These children seldom started
conversations with teachers or other students, but they
would sometimes answer questions with a word or
perhaps two. This pattern may be unusual in the middle
classes, but is quite common among ghetto children.
Our research has shown that children so afflicted are
usually uneducable.

As we investigated, we became convinced that their problem was not that they were unable to talk as much as that they were too shy to talk to strangers—that is, to nonfamily. In their homes we overheard most of them talking brokenly, but in sentences. Consequently, we set up a token exchange for them designed specifically to develop a pattern of talking with outsiders, especially teachers and school children.

As it happened, we were able to complete the experiment with only four children (see Figure 6). During A1, the baseline period (before the tokens were used), the four children spoke only in about 8 percent of the 15-second sampling periods. In B1, the teachers gave social approval and tokens *only* for speaking; nonverbalisms, like pointing or headshaking, would not be recognized or reinforced. Note the increase in verbalization, leveling out at approximately 48 percent.

In A2 we reversed the conditions by using a teacher new to the school. The rate of talking dropped off immediately, then increased unevenly until it occurred in about 23 percent of the sample periods.

In B2 the new teacher reintroduced the token exchange for talking, and once more there was a dramatic rise: The speaking increased much more rapidly than the first time, ending up at about 60 percent. (This more rapid increase is known as the Contrast Effect. It occurs in part, perhaps, because the children value the token exchange more after it has been taken away.)

In the final test, we again took out the token exchange, and introduced yet another new teacher. This time the drop was small, to 47 percent.

We followed the children for three months after the end of the experiment. Their speech level remained at

48 percent, with little dropoff. This compares with the 40 percent talking rate for our other ghetto children, and the 42 percent rate for upper-middle-class children at the Washington University pre-school.

Frequency of speech, however, was not the only important finding. At the end of B1, the children spoke more often but still in a hesitant and broken way. By the end of B2, they spoke in sentences, used better syntax, and frequently started conversations.

Mothers, teachers and neighbors all reported that the children were much more friendly and assertive. But some claimed that the children now talked too much! This could reflect individual bias; but there was little doubt that at least one child, Ben, had become an almost compulsive talker. He was given to saying hello to everyone he met and shaking their hands. So we terminated the experiment—what would have happened to Ben had we started *another* exchange?

This experiment shows that token exchange can bring on permanent behavior change, but that the culture must reinforce the new behavior. Talking is important in our culture, and so is reading; therefore they are reinforced. But other subjects—such as mathematics beyond simple arithmetic—are not important for most people. For behavior to change permanently it must be reinforced at least intermittently.

The problems of autistic children usually dwarf those of all other children. To the casual observer, autistic children never sustain eye contact with others but appear to be self-contained—sealed off in a world of their own. The most severe cases never learn how to talk, though they sometimes echo or parrot. They remain dependent upon Mother and become more and more demanding. They develop increasingly destructive

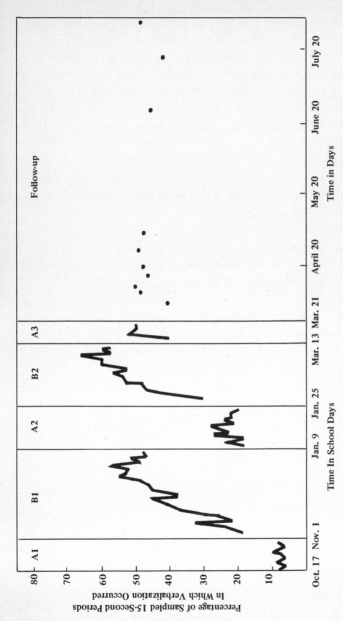

Figure 6. Percentage of sampled periods in which talking occured through time for four non-verbal "culturally deprived" children, and through five experimental conditions. In each of the A conditions a new teacher was introduced, and she structured a token exchange for participation in lessons. In the B conditions, the teacher then structured a token exchange for talking. The follow-up was similar to the A conditions.

and bizarre behavior problems. Finally, between five
and ten years old, autistic children ordinarily become
unbearable to their families and at that point they are
almost invariably institutionalized. Until recently, at
least, this meant a rear ward to vegetate in until they
died.

The breakthrough in therapy from autism came in
1964 when Ivar Lovaas and Montrose Wolfe and a
graduate student, Todd Risley, simultaneously developed therapy systems using well-established principles
of operant conditioning. They were particularly successful with those children who randomly echoed or
imitated words or sentences (this is called echolalia).

The therapy systems we have designed, developed and
tested, though similar in some ways to those developed
by Lovaas, Wolfe and Risley, are quite different in
others. First, we do not use punishment, or other
negative stimuli. We simply terminate exchanges that
reinforce the autistic patterns, and set up exchanges that
reinforce normal patterns. Second, our children are not
institutionalized; they live at home, and are brought to
the laboratory for 20 minutes to three hours of therapy
per day. Third, as soon as possible—usually within
months—we get the children into classrooms where a
therapist works with four or five at a time. Fourth, we
train the mother to be an assistant therapist—mostly in
the home, but also in the laboratory. These changes
were introduced for several reasons, but primarily in the
hope of getting a better, more permanent cure for
autism.

Is autism hereditary, as many believe? Our studies
indicate that this is not the important question. Many
mental faculties, including IQ, have some physiological
base. But the real issue is how much physiologically

based potential is socially realized, for good or bad. As far as we can tell, the exchanges that intensify autism get structured inadvertently, often by accident; but once started, a vicious cycle develops that relentlessly drives the child further into autism.

When autism starts, the mother often reacts by babying the child, trying to anticipate his every need before he signals. Thus normal communication is not reinforced, and the child never learns to work his environment properly. But even if he doesn't know how to get what he wants through talking, he does learn, through association, that his oversolicitous and anxious mother will always respond if he acts up violently or bizarrely enough. And she must, if only to punish. He thus learns to play "Get Mother's attention"; and this soon develops into "Get Mother exasperated, but stop just short of the point where she punishes and really hurts." Here is an example (observed by Ferritor in the first of a series of experiments by the Laboratory's staff, not reported here):

Larry is allowed to pick out his favorite book. His mother then attempts to read it to him, but he keeps turning the pages so she can't. He gets up and walks away from the table. The mother then yells at him to come back. He *smiles* (a sign of pleasure usually, but not always, accompanies reinforcement). Mother continues to talk to the child to try to get him back for the story. Finally, he comes over to the table and takes the book away from her. She lets him and goes back to the bookcase for another book. He then sits down and she begins to read. He tries to get up, but his mother pulls him back. Again. Again. She holds him there. He gets away and starts walking around the room. Goes to the toy cabinet. Mother gets up to go over and take a toy away from him. He sits on the floor. The mother comes over and sits down by him. He gets up and goes over by the door and opens it and tries to run out. She tells him he has to stay. He *smiles.* She resumes reading. He gets up and starts walking around the table. She grabs him as he comes by. He *smiles.*

A clinical psychologist who had tested Larry did not diagnose him as autistic, but as an educable mental retardate with an IQ of perhaps 30. Yet he had gaze aversion and we suspected that Larry, like other autistics, was feigning inability as a way of getting what he wanted from his mother, and then from other adults. He began to respond to the attractive exchanges that we structured for him, and as we did, he began to tip his hand. For example, at one point when his mother was being trained to be an assistant therapist, the following incident occurred:

Mrs. C. told Larry that as soon as he strung some beads he could have gum from the gum machine that was across the room. For about ten minutes he fumbled, he whined, all the time crying, saying "I can't." Finally, he threw the beads at his mother. Eventually, the mother had the good sense to leave the room, saying, "As soon as you string those beads, you can have your gum." With his mother out of the room, according to our observers he sat right down and, in less than 30 seconds, filled a string with beads with no apparent trouble.

Just two weeks later, after the mother had been through our ten-day training program, they again had a "story time."

The mother begins by immediately asking Larry questions about this book (the same book used a few weeks before). He responds to every question. She gives approval for every correct answer. Then she tries to get him to say, "That is a duck." He will not say it intelligibly, but wants to turn the page. Mother says, "As soon as you say 'duck,' you may turn the page. Larry says "Duck" and turns the page. He *smiles.*

After seven minutes, Larry is still sitting down. They have finished one book and are beginning a second.

Most autistic children play the game "Look at me, I'm stupid," or "Look at me, I'm bizarre." These are simply attention-getting games that most adults repeatedly reinforce. Man is not a simple machine; he learns, and as he develops his abilities, he develops stronger and stronger habits. Thus, once these inadvertent exchanges get established, the child becomes more and more dependent, more and more disruptive, more and more bizarre, more and more alienated from the positive exchanges that are structured in his environment. What is sad is that the parents and the others in the child's life sense that something is terribly wrong, but the more they do, the worse the situation becomes.

It seems to those of us who have been involved in these experiments from the beginning that the exchange techniques and theories we have used have without question demonstrated their effectiveness in treating and educating problem children. Watching these children as they go peacefully and productively about their lessons toward the end of each experimental series is both an exhilarating and humbling experience. It is almost impossible to believe that so many had been written off as "uneducable" by professionals, that without this therapy and training—or something similar—most would have had dark and hopeless futures.

But it is not inevitable that so many hyperaggressive or environmentally retarded ghetto children become dropouts or delinquents; it is not inevitable that so many autistic children, saddest of all, must vegetate and die mutely in the back wards of mental hospitals.

January 1969

FURTHER READING:

The Analysis of Human Operant Behavior by Ellen P. Reese (Dubuque Iowa: William C. Brown Company, 1966).

The Emotionally Disturbed Child in the Classroom by Frank Hewett (Boston: Allyn and Bacon, Inc., 1968).

Early Childhood Autism edited by J.K. Wing (London: Pergamon Press, Ltd., 1966).

Case Studies in Behavior Modification by Leonard P. Ullman and Leonard Krasner (New York: Holt, Rinehart and Winston, Inc., 1965).

Note: The work reported here was done by the Central Midwestern Regional Educational Laboratory, a private, non-profit corporation supported in part as a Regional Educational Laboratory by funds from the U.S. Office of Education, Department of Health, Education and Welfare. The opinions expressed here do not necessarily reflect the position or policy of the Office of Education, and no official endorsement by the Office of Education should be inferred.

Programmed for Social Class: Tracking in American High Schools

WALTER E. SCHAEFER
CAROL OLEXA and KENNETH POLK

If, as folklore would have it, America is the land of opportunity, offering anyone the chance to raise himself purely on the basis of his or her ability, then education is the key to self-betterment. The spectacular increase in those of us who attend school is often cited as proof of the great scope of opportunity that our society offers: 94 percent of the high school age population was attending school in 1967, as compared to 7 percent in 1890.

Similarly, our educational system is frequently called more democratic than European systems, for instance, which rigidly segregate students by ability early in their lives, often on the basis of nationally administered examinations such as England's "11-plus." The United States, of course, has no official national policy of educational segregation. Our students, too, are tested and retested throughout their lives and put into faster or slower classes or programs on the basis of their presumed ability, but this procedure is carried out in a decentralized fashion that varies between each city or state.

However, many critics of the American practice claim that, no matter how it is carried out, it does not meet the needs of the brighter and duller groups, so much as it solidifies and widens the differences between them. One such critic, the eminent educator Kenneth B. Clark, speculates: "It is conceivable that the detrimental effects of segregation based upon intellect are similar to the known detrimental effects of schools segregated on the basis of class, nationality or race."

Patricia Cayo Sexton notes that school grouping based on presumed ability often reinforces already existing social divisions:

Children from higher social strata usually enter the "higher quality" groups and those from lower strata the "lower" ones. School decisions about a child's ability will greatly influeence the kind and quality of education he receives, as well as his future life, including whether he goes to college, the job he will get, and his feelings about himself and others.

And Arthur Pearl puts it bluntly:

... "special ability classes," "basic track," or "slow learner classes" are various names for another means of systematically denying the poor adequate access to education.

In this chapter we will examine some evidence bearing on this vital question of whether current educational practices tend to reinforce existing social class divisions. We will also offer an alternative aimed at making our public schools more effective institutions for keeping open the opportunities for social mobility.

Since the turn of the century, a number of trends have converged to increase enormously the pressure on American adolescents to graduate from high school: declining opportunity in jobs, the upgrading of educational requirements for job entry, and the diminishing need for teenagers to contribute to family income. While some school systems, especially in the large cities, have adapted to this vast increase in enrollment by creating separate high schools for students with different interests, abilities or occupational goals, most communities have developed comprehensive high schools serving all the youngsters within a neighborhood or community.

In about half the high schools in the United States today, the method for handling these large and varied student populations is through some form of tracking system. Under this arrangement, the entire student body is divided into two or more relatively distinct career lines, or tracks, with such titles as college preparatory, vocational, technical, industrial, business, general, basic and remedial. While students on different tracks may take some courses together in the same classroom, they are usually separated into entirely different courses or different sections of the same course.

Schoolmen offer several different justifications for tracking systems. Common to most, however, is the notion that college-bound students are academically more able, learn more rapidly, should not be deterred in their progress by slower, non-college-bound students, and need courses for college preparation which non-college-bound students do not need. By the same token, it is thought that non-college-bound students are less bright, learn more slowly, should not be expected to progress as fast or learn as much as college-bound students, and need only a general education or work-oriented training to prepare themselves for immediate entry into the world of work or a business or vocational school.

In reply, the numerous critics of tracking usually contend that while the college-bound are often encouraged by the tracking system to improve their performance, non-college-bound students, largely as a result of being placed in a lower-rated track, are discouraged from living up to their potential or from showing an interest in academic values. What makes the system especially pernicious, these critics say, is that non-college-bound students more often come from low-income and minority group families. As a result, high schools, through the tracking system, inadvertently close off opportunities for large numbers of students from lower social strata, and thereby contribute to the low achievement, lack of interest, delinquency and rebellion which schoolmen frequently deplore in their noncollege track students.

If these critics are correct, the American comprehensive high school, which is popularly assumed to be the very model of an open and democratic institution, may not really be open and democratic at all. In fact, rather than facilitating equality of educational opportunity, our schools may be subtly denying it, and in the process widening and hardening existing social divisions.

During the summer of 1964, we collected data from official school transcripts of the recently graduated senior classes of two midwestern three-year high schools. The larger school, located in a predominantly middle-class, academic community of about 70,000, had a graduating class that year of 753 students. The smaller school, with a graduating class of 404, was located nearby in a predominantly working-class, industrial community of about 20,000.

Both schools placed their students into either a college prep or general track. We determined the positions of every student in our sample by whether he took tenth grade English in the college prep or the general section. If he was enrolled in the college prep section, he almost always took other college prep sections or courses, such as advanced mathematics or foreign languages, in which almost all enrollees were also college prep.

Just how students in the two schools were assigned to—or chose—tracks is somewhat of a mystery. When we interviewed people both in the high schools and in their feeder junior highs, we were told that whether a student went into one track or another depended on various factors, such as his own desires and aspirations, teacher advice, achievement test scores, grades, pressure from parents and counselor assessment of academic promise. One is hard put to say which of these weighs most heavily, but we must note that one team of researchers, Cicourel and Kitsuse, showed in their study of *The Educational Decision-Makers* that assumptions made by counselors about the character, adjustment and potential of incoming students are vitally important in track assignment.

Whatever the precise dynamics of this decision, the outcome was clear in the schools we studied: socioeconomic and racial background had an effect on which track a student took, quite apart from either his achievement in junior high or his ability as measured by IQ scores. In the smaller, working-class school, 58 percent of the incoming students were assigned to the college prep track; in the larger, middle-class school, 71 percent were placed in the college prep track. And, taking the two schools together, whereas 83 percent of students from white-collar homes were assigned to the college prep track, this was the case with only 48 percent of students from blue-collar homes. The relationship of race to track assignment was even stronger: 71 percent of the whites and only 30 percent of the blacks were assigned to the college prep track. In the two schools studied, the evidence is plain: Children from low income and minority group families more often found themselves in low ability groups and non-college-bound tracks than in high ability groups or college-bound tracks.

Furthermore, this decision-point early in the students' high school careers was of great significance for their futures, since it was virtually irreversible. Only 7 percent of those who began on the college prep track moved down to the noncollege prep track, while only 7 percent of those assigned to the lower, noncollege track, moved up. Clearly, these small figures indicate a high degree of rigid segregation within each of the two schools. In fact, greater mobility between levels has been reported in English secondary modern schools, where streaming—the British term for tracking—is usually thought to be more rigid and fixed than tracking in this country. (It must be remembered, of course, that in England the more rigid break is between secondary modern and grammar schools.)

As might be expected from the schoolmen's justification for placing students in separate tracks in the first place, track position is noticeably related to academic performance. Thirty-seven percent of the college prep students graduated in the top quarter of their class (measured by grade point average throughout high school), while a mere 2 percent of the noncollege group achieved the top quarter. By contrast, half the non-college prep students fell in the lowest quarter, as opposed to only 12 percent of the college prep.

Track position is also strikingly related to whether a student's academic performance improves or deterio-rates during high school. The grade point average of all sample students in their ninth year—that is, prior to their being assigned to tracks—was compared with their grade point averages over the next three years. While there was a slight difference in the ninth year between those who would subsequently enter the college and noncollege tracks, this difference had increased by the senior year. This widening gap in academic performance resulted from the fact that a higher percentage of students subsequently placed in the college prep track improved their grade point average by the senior year, while a higher percentage of noncollege prep experi-enced a decline in grade point average by the time they reached the senior year.

Track position is also related strongly to dropout rate. Four percent of the college prep students dropped out of high school prior to graduation, as opposed to 36 percent of the noncollege group.

Track position is also a good indication of how deeply involved a student will be in school, as measured by participation in extracurricular activities. Out of the 753 seniors in the larger school, a comparatively small number of college prep students—21 percent—did not participate in any activities, while 44 percent took part in three or more such activities. By contrast, 58 percent, or more than half of the noncollege group took part in no extracurricular activities at all, and only 11 percent of this group took part in three or more activities.

Finally, track position is strikingly related to delinquency, both in and out of school. Out of the entire
student body of the larger school who committed one
or more violations during the 1963-1964 school year,
just over one-third were college-bound, while just over
one-half were non-college-bound. (The track position of
the remaining one-tenth was unknown.) Among those
who committed three or more such violations, 19
percent were college-bound, compared with 70 percent
who were non-college-bound. Among all those suspend-
ed, over one-third were college-bound, while just over
one-half were non-college-bound. In short, the non-
college-bound students were considerably more often
caught and sanctioned for violations of school rules,
even though they comprised less than one-third of the
student body.

Furthermore, using juvenile court records, we find
that out of the 1964 graduating class in the larger
school, 6 percent of the college prep, and 16 percent of
the non-college-bound groups, were delinquent while in
high school. Even though 5 percent of those on the
noncollege track had already entered high school with
court records, opposed to only 1 percent of the college
prep track, still more non-college-bound students became delinquent during high school than did college
prep students (11 percent compared with 5 percent). So
the relation between track position and delinquency is
further supported.

We have seen, then, that when compared with college
prep students, noncollege prep students show lower
achievement, great deterioration of achievement, less
participation in extracurricular activities, a greater tendency to drop out, more misbehavior in school, and more
delinquency outside of school. Since students are

assigned to different tracks largely on the basis of presumed differences in intellectual ability and inclination for study, the crucial question is whether assignment to different tracks helped to meet the needs of groups of students who were already different, as many educators would claim, or actually contributed to and reinforced such differences, as critics like Sexton and Pearl contend.

The simplest way to explain the differences we have just seen is to attribute them to characteristics already inherent in the individual students, or—at a more sophisticated level—to students' cultural and educational backgrounds.

It can be argued, for example, that the difference in academic achievement between the college and non-college groups can be explained by the fact that college prep students are simply brighter; after all, this is one of the reasons they were taken into college prep courses. Others would argue that non-college-bound students do less well in school work because of family background: they more often come from blue-collar homes where less value is placed on grades and college, where books and help in schoolwork are less readily available, and verbal expression limited. Still others would contend that lower track students get lower grades because they performed less well in elementary and junior high, have fallen behind, and probably try less hard.

Fortunately, it was possible with our data to separate out the influence of track position from the other suggested factors of social class background (measured by father's occupation), intelligence (measured by IQ—admittedly not a perfectly acceptable measure), and previous academic performance (measured by grade point average for the last semester of the ninth year).

Through use of a weighted percentage technique known as test factor standardization, we found that even when the effects of IQ, social class and previous performance are ruled out, there is still a sizable difference in grade point average between the two tracks. With the influence of the first three factors eliminated we nevertheless find that 30 percent of the college prep, as opposed to a mere 4 percent of the noncollege group attained the top quarter of their class; and that only 12 percent of the college prep, as opposed to 35 percent of the noncollege group, fell into the bottom quarter. These figures, which are similar for boys and girls, further show that track position has an independent effect on academic achievement which is greater than the effect of each of the other three factors—social class, IQ and past performance. In particular, assignment to the noncollege track has a strong negative influence on a student's grades.

Looking at dropout rate, and again controlling for social class background, IQ and past performance, we find that track position in itself has an independent influence which is higher than the effect of any of the other three factors. In other words, even when we rule out the effect of these three factors, non-college-bound students still dropped out in considerably greater porportion than college-bound-students (19 percent vs. 4 percent).

So our evidence points to the conclusion that the superior academic performance of the college-bound students, and the inferior performance of the noncollege students is partly caused by the tracking system. Our data do not explain how this happens, but several studies of similar educational arrangements, as well as basic principles of social psychology do provide a

number of probable explanations. The first point has to
do with the pupil's self-image.

Stigma. Assignment to the lower track in the schools
we studied carried with it a strong stigma. As David
Mallory was told by an American boy, "Around here
you are *nothing* if you're not college prep." A noncollege prep girl in one of the schools we studied told
me that she always carried her "general" track books
upside down because of the humiliation she felt at being
seen with them as she walked through the halls.

The corroding effect of such stigmatizing is well
known. As Patricia Sexton has put it, "He [the low
track student] is bright enough to catch on very quickly
to the fact that he is not considered very bright. He
comes to accept this unflattering appraisal because, after
all, the school should know."

One ex-delinquent in Washington, D.C. told one of us
how the stigma from this low track affected him.

It really don't have to be the tests, but after the tests,
there shouldn't be no separation in the classes.
Because, as I say again, I felt good when I was with
my class, but when they went and separated us—that
changed us. That changed our ideas, our thinking, the
way we thought about each other and turned us to
enemies toward each other—because they said I was
dumb and they were smart. When you first go to
junior high school you do feel something inside—it's
like ego. You have been from elementary to junior
high, you feel great inside. You say, well daggone, I'm
going to deal with the *people* here now, I am in junior
high school. You get this shirt that says Brown Junior
High or whatever the name is and you are proud of
that shirt. But then you go up there and the teacher
says—"Well, so and so, you're in the basic section,

you can't go with the other kids." The devil with the whole thing—you lose—something in you—like it just goes out of you.

Did you think the other guys were smarter than you? Not at first—I used to think I was just as smart as anybody in the school—I knew I was smart. I knew some people were smarter, and I *wanted* to go to school, I wanted to get a diploma and go to college and help people and everything. I stepped into there in junior high—I felt like a fool going to school—I really felt like a fool. *Why?* Because I felt like I wasn't a part of the school. I couldn't get on special patrols, because I wasn't qualified.

What happened between the seventh and ninth grades? I started losing faith in myself—after the teachers kept downing me. You hear "a guy's in basic section, he's dumb" and all this. Each year—"you're ignorant—you're stupid."

Considerable research shows that such erosion of self-esteem greatly increases the chances of academic failure, as well as dropping out and causing "trouble" both inside and outside of school.

Moreover, this lowered self-image is reinforced by the expectations that others have toward a person in the non-college-bound group.

The Self-fulfilling Prophecy. A related explanation rich in implications comes from David Hargreaves' *Social Relations in a Secondary School*, a study of the psychological, behavioral and educational consequences of the student's position in the streaming system of an English secondary modern school. In "Lumley School," the students (all boys) were assigned to one of five streams on the basis of ability and achievement, with the score on the "11-plus" examination playing the major role.

Like the schools we studied, students in the different streams were publicly recognized as high or low in status and were fairly rigidly segregated, both formally in different classes and informally in friendship groups. It is quite probable, then, that Hargreaves' explanations for the greater antischool attitudes, animosity toward teachers, academic failure, disruptive behavior and delinquency among the low stream boys apply to the noncollege prep students we studied as well. In fact, the negative effects of the tracking system on non-college-bound students may be even stronger in our two high schools, since the Lumley streaming system was much more open and flexible, with students moving from one stream to another several times during their four-year careers.

As we noted, a popular explanation for the greater failure and misbehavior among low stream or non-college-bound students is that they come from homes that fail to provide the same skills, ambition or conforming attitude as higher stream or college-bound students. Hargreaves demonstrates that there is some validity to this position: in his study, low stream boys more often came from homes that provided less encouragement for academic achievement and higher level occupations, and that were less oriented to the other values of the school and teachers. Similar differences may have existed among the students we studied, although their effects have been markedly reduced by our control for father's occupation, IQ and previous achievement.

But Hargreaves provides a convincing case for the

position that whatever the differences in skills, ambition, self-esteem or educational commitment that the students brought to school, they were magnified by what happened to them in school, largely because low stream boys were the victims of a self-fulfilling prophecy in their relations with teachers, with respect to both academic performance and classroom behavior. Teachers of higher stream boys expected higher performance and got it. Similarly, boys who wore the label of streams "C" or "D" were more likely to be seen by teachers as limited in ability and troublemakers, and were treated accordingly.

In a streamed school the teacher categorizes the pupils not only in terms of the inferences he makes of the child's class room behavior but also from the child's stream level. It is for this reason that the teacher can rebuke an "A" stream boy for being like a "D" stream boy. The teacher has learned to *expect* certain kinds of behavior from members of different streams. . . . It would be hardly surprising if "good" pupils thus became "better" and the "bad" pupils become "worse." It is, in short, an example of a self-fulfilling prophecy. The negative expectations of the teacher reinforce the negative behavioral tendencies.

A recent study by Rosenthal and Jacobson in an American elementary school lends further evidence to the position that teacher expectations influence student's performance. In this study, the influence is a positive one. Teachers of children randomly assigned to experimental groups were told at the beginning of the year to expect "unusual intellectual" gains, while teachers of the control group children were told nothing. After eight months, and again after two years, the experimental group children, the "intellectual spurt-ers," showed significantly greater gains in IQ and grades. Further, they were rated by the teachers as being significantly more curious, interesting, happy and more likely to succeed in the future. Such findings are consistent with theories of interpersonal influence and with the interactional or labelling view of deviant behavior.

If, as often claimed, American teachers underestimate the learning potential of low track students and expect more negative attitudes and greater trouble from them, it may well be that they partially cause the very failure, alienation, lack of involvement, dropping out and rebellion they are seeking to prevent. As Hargreaves says of Lumley, "It is important to stress that if this effect of categorization is real, it is entirely unintended by the teachers. They do not wish to make low streams more difficult than they are!" Yet the negative self-fulfilling prophecy was probably real, if unintended and unrecognized, in our two schools as well as in Lumley.

Two further consequences of the expectation that students in the noncollege group will learn less well are differences in grading policies and in teacher effectiveness.

Grading Policies. In the two schools we studied, our interviews strongly hint at the existence of grade ceilings for noncollege prep students and grade floors for college-bound students. That is, by virtue of being located in a college preparatory section or course, college prep students could seldom receive any grade lower than "B" or "C," while students in non-college-bound sections or courses found it difficult to gain any grade higher than "C," even though their objective performance may have been equivalent to a college prep

"B." Several teachers explicitly called our attention to this practice, the rationale being that noncollege prep students do not deserve the same objective grade rewards as college prep students, since they "clearly" are less bright and perform less well. To the extent that grade ceilings do operate for non-college-bound students, the lower grades that result from this policy, almost by definition, can hardly have a beneficial effect on motivation and commitment.

Teaching Effectiveness. Finally, numerous investigations of ability grouping, as well as the English study by Hargreaves, have reported that teachers of higher ability groups are likely to teach in a more interesting and effective manner than teachers of lower ability groups. Such a difference is predictable from what we know about the effects of reciprocal interaction between teacher and class. Even when the same individual teaches both types of classes in the course of the day, as was the case for most teachers in the two schools in this study, he is likely to be "up" for college prep classes and "down" for noncollege prep classes—and to bring out the same reaction from his students.

A final and crucial factor that contributes to the poorer performance and lower interest in school of non-college-bound students is the relation between school work and the adult career after school.

Future Payoff. Non-college-bound students often develop progressively more negative attitudes toward school, especially formal academic work, because they see grades—and indeed school itself—as having little future relevance or payoff. This is not the case for college prep students. For them, grades are a means toward the identifiable and meaningful end of qualifying for college, while among the non-college-bound, grades are seen as far less important for entry into an occupation or a vocational school. This difference in the practical importance of grades is magnified by the perception among non-college-bound students that it is pointless to put much effort into school work, since it will be unrelated to the later world of work anyway. In a study of *Rebellion in a High School* in this country, Arthur Stinchcombe describes the alienation of non-college-bound high school students:

> The major practical conclusion of the analysis above is that rebellious behavior is largely a reaction to the school itself and to its promises, not a failure of the family or community. High school students can be motivated to conform by paying them in the realistic coin of future advantage. Except perhaps for pathological cases, any student can be motivated to conform if the school can realistically promise something valuable to him as a reward for working hard. But for a large part of the population, especially the adolescent who will enter the male working class or the female candidates for early marriage, the school has nothing to offer. . . . In order to secure conformity from students, a high school must articulate academic work with careers of students.

Being on the lower track has other negative consequences for the student which go beyond the depressing influence on his academic performance and motivation. We can use the principles just discussed to explain our findings with regard to different rates of participation in school activities and acts of misbehavior.

For example, the explanations having to do with self-image and the expectations of others suggest that assignment to the non-college-bound track has a dampening effect on commitment to school in general, since it is the school which originally categorized these students as inferior. Thus, assignment to the lower track may be seen as independently contributing to resentment, frustration and hostility in school, leading to lack of involvement in all school activities, and finally ending in active withdrawal. The self-exclusion of the non-college group from the mainstream of college student life is probably enhanced by intentional or unintentional exclusion by other students and teachers.

Using the same type of reasons, while we cannot prove a definite causal linkage between track position and misbehavior, it seems highly likely that assignment to the non-college prep track often leads to resentment, declining commitment to school, and rebellion against it, expressed in lack of respect for the school's authority or acts of disobedience against it. As Albert Cohen argued over a decade ago in *Delinquent Boys,* delinquency may well be largely a rebellion against the school and its standards by teenagers who feel they cannot get anywhere by attempting to adhere to such standards. Our analysis suggests that a key factor in such rebellion is noncollege prep status in the school's tracking system, with the vicious cycle of low achievement and inferior self-image that go along with it.

This conclusion is further supported by Hargreaves' findings on the effect of streaming at Lumley:

There is a real sense in which the school can be regarded as a generator of delinquency. Although the aims and efforts of the teachers are directed towards deleting such tendencies, the organization of the school and its influence on subcultural development unintentionally fosters delinquent values. . . . For low stream boys . . . school simultaneously exposes them to these values and deprives them of status in these terms. It is at this point they may begin to reject the values because they cannot succeed in them. The school provides a mechanism through the streaming system whereby their failure is effected and institutionalized, and also provides a situation in which they can congregate together in low streams.

Hargreaves' last point suggests a very important explanation for the greater degree of deviant behavior among the non-college-bound.

The Student Subculture. Assignment to a lower stream at Lumley meant a boy was immediately immersed in a student subculture that stressed and rewarded antagonistic attitudes and behavior toward teachers and all they stood for. If a boy was assigned to the "A" stream, he was drawn toward the values of teachers, not only by the higher expectations and more positive rewards from the teachers themselves, but from other students as well. The converse was true of lower stream boys, who accorded each other high status for doing the opposite of what teachers wanted. Because of class scheduling, little opportunity developed for interaction and friendship across streams. The result was a progressive polarization and hardening of the high and low stream subcultures between first and fourth years and a progressively greater negative attitude across stream lines, with quite predictable consequences.

The informal pressures within the low streams tend to work directly against the assumption of the teachers that boys will regard promotion into a higher stream as a desirable goal. The boys from the low streams were very reluctant to ascend to higher streams because their stereotypes of "A" and "B" stream boys were defined in terms of values alien to their own and because promotion would involve rejection by their low stream friends. The teachers were not fully aware that this unwillingness to be promoted to a higher stream led the high informal status boys to depress their performance in examinations. This fear of promotion adds to our list of factors leading to the formation of anti-academic attitudes among low stream boys.

Observations and interviews in the two American schools we studied confirmed a similar polarization and reluctance by noncollege prep students to pursue the academic goals rewarded by teachers and college prep students. Teachers, however, seldom saw the antischool attitudes of noncollege prep students as arising out of the tracking system—or anything else about the school—but out of adverse home influences, limited intelligence or psychological problems.

Implications. These, then, are some of the ways the schools we studied contributed to the greater rates of failure, academic decline, uninvolvement in school activities, misbehavior and delinquency among non-college-bound students. We can only speculate, of course, about the generalizability of these findings to other schools. However, there is little reason to think that the two schools we studied were unusual or unrepresentative and, despite differences in size and social class composition, the findings are virtually identical in both—and are consistent with the speculations, criticisms and unsystematic observations of numerous writers. To the extent the findings are valid and general, they strongly suggest that, through their tracking system, the schools are partly causing many of the very problems they are trying to solve and are posing an important barrier to equal educational opportunity to lower income and black students, who are disproportionately assigned to the non-college prep track. The notion that schools help cause low achievement, deterioration of educational commitment and involvement, the dropout problem, misbehavior and delinquency is foreign and repulsive to many teachers, administrators and parents. Yet our evidence is entirely consistent with Kai Erikson's observation that "...deviant forms of conduct often seem to derive nourishment from the very agencies devised to inhibit them."

What, then, are the implications from this study? Some might argue that, despite the negative side effects we have shown, tracking systems are essential for effective teaching, especially for students with high ability, as well as for adjusting students early in their careers to the status levels they will occupy in the adult occupational system. We contend that however reasonable this may sound, the negative effects demonstrated here offset and call into serious question any presumed gains from tracking.

Others might contend that the negative outcomes we have documented can be eliminated by raising teachers' expectations of non-college track students, making concerted efforts to reduce the stigma attached to noncollege classes, assigning good teachers to non-college track classes, rewarding them for doing an effective job at turning on their students, and developing fair and equitable grading practices in both college prep and non-college prep classes.

Attractive as they may appear, efforts like these will be fruitless, so long as tracking systems, and indeed schools as we now know them, remain unchanged. What is needed are wholly new, experimental environments of teaching-learning-living, even outside today's public schools, if necessary. Such schools of the future must address themselves to two sets of problems highlighted by our findings: ensuring equality of opportunity for students now "locked out" by tracking, and offering—to all students—a far more fulfilling and satisfying learning process.

One approach to building greater equality of opportunity, as well as fulfillment, into existing or new secondary schools is the New Careers model. This model, which provides for fundamentally different linkages between educational and occupational careers, is based on the recognition that present options for entering the world of work are narrowly limited: one acquires a high school diploma and goes to work, or he first goes to college and perhaps then to a graduate or professional school. (Along the way, of course, young men must cope with the draft.)

The New Careers model provides for new options. Here the youth who does not want to attend college or would not qualify according to usual criteria, is given the opportunity to attend high school part-time while working in a lower level position in an expanded professional career hierarchy (including such new positions as teacher aide and teacher associate in education). Such a person would then have the options of moving up through progressively more demanding educational and work stages; and moving back and forth between the work place, the high school and then the college. As ideally conceived, this model would allow able and aspiring persons ultimately to progress to the level of the fully certified teacher, nurse, librarian, social worker, or public administrator. While the New Careers model has been developed and tried primarily in the human service sector of the economy, we have pointed out elsewhere that it is also applicable to the industrial and business sector as well. (See Walter E. Schafer and Kenneth Polk, "Delinquency and the Schools," *Task Force Report: Juvenile Delinquency and Youth Crime:* The President's Commission on Law Enforcement and Administration of Justice, U.S. Government Printing Office, 1967.)

This alternative means of linking education with work has a number of advantages: students can try different occupations while still in school; students can earn while studying; they can spend more time outside the four walls of the school, learning what can best be learned in the work place; less stigma will accrue to those not immediately college-bound, since they too will have a future; studying and learning will be inherently more relevant because it will relate to a career in which they are actively involved; teachers of such students will be less likely to develop lower expectations because these youth too will have an unlimited, open-ended future; and antischool subcultures will be less likely to develop, since education will not be as negative, frustrating or stigmatizing.

To ensure equality of opportunity is not enough. Merely to open the channels for lower income youth to flow into educational careers that are now turning off millions of middle class, college-bound youth is hardly doing anyone a favor. Though not reflected in our data, many middle class students now find school even less tolerable than do low income youth. The empty grade-scrambling, teacher-pleasing and stultifying passivity such youth must endure stands in greater and greater contrast to their home and other non-school environments which usually yield much greater excitement, challenge and reward. More and more are dropping out psychologically, turning instead to drugs, apathy or political activism, often of an unthinking and self-defeating kind.

What is needed, then are entirely new and different models that will assure not only equality of opportunity but also much more in the way of an enriching and rewarding growth process. Educational environments of the future, incorporating New Careers as well as other new forms, must follow several simple guidelines.

First, successful new learning environments must be based on the recognition and acceptance of each individual's uniqueness. Each person must be allowed and stimulated to develop, learn and grow as an individual, not as a standardized occupant of any gross human category. As Kenneth Keniston stated in *The Uncommitted,* "Human diversity and variety must not only be tolerated, but rejoiced in, applauded, and encouraged."

At the beginning, we pointed out that tracking was an educational response to the increased pupil diversity created by pressure on adolescents from employers, parents and educators themselves to stay in school longer. While it may be an efficient way to screen large numbers of youth out of the educational and economic systems, and while it may be bureaucratically convenient, tracking is crude at best and destructive at worst in psychological and educational terms. Predictably, the occupants of the categories created by tracking come to be perceived, treated and taught according to what they are thought to have in common: college material or not college material, bright or not bright, motivated or not motivated, fast or not fast. Yet psychologists of individual differences and learning have told us for years what every parent already knows from common sense and experience: each child is unique in aptitudes, style of interaction, learning style and rate, energy level, interests, self-attitudes, reactions to challenge and stress, and in countless other ways. New educational environments must be adaptable to these differences.

The second guideline must be that the potential for individual growth and development is virtually unlimited and must be freed and stimulated to develop as fully as possible during each student's lifetime. We must stop assuming human potential is somehow fixed or circumscribed. Tragically, tracking—and indeed the whole structure of schooling—is founded on this premise. George Leonard puts it well in his *Education and Ecstacy:* ". . .the task of *preventing* the new generation from changing in any deep or significant way is precisely what most societies require of their educators." Not surprisingly, then, "The most obvious barrier between our children and the kind of education that can free their enormous potential seems to be the educational system itself: a vast, suffocating web of people, practices, and presumptions, kindly in intent, ponderous in response." In building new environments for becoming—with rich and limitless opportunities for exploration into self and others, other places, times and ideas, and the unknown—educators can play a part in seeing to it that more than today's mere fraction of potential learning and growing is unleashed.

The third guideline must be that "learning is sheer delight," to quote Leonard. For the non-college bound—indeed for the vast majority, including neat and tidy "high achievers"—"schooling" (we can hardly call it learning) is the very opposite. Tragically, Leonard may be all too right: "A visitor from another planet might conclude that our schools are hell-bent on creating—in a society that offers leisure and demands creativity—a generation of joyless drudges . . .when joy is absent, the effectiveness of the learning process falls and falls until the human being is operating hesitantly, grudgingly, fearfully at only a tiny fraction of his potential." For joy to enter learning, "cognitive learning" must be reunited with affective, physical and behavioral growth. The payoff must be now. Will learning then stop with the diploma?

If new learning-teaching-living environments follow these simple guidelines, not only will the negative effects of tracking be eliminated, but several features of the student role that alienate all types of students can also be avoided: passivity, subordination, forced separation from self, fragmented sequencing of learning, age segregation, isolation from community life with the unrealities of school that follow, an almost exclusive instrumental emphasis on future gains from schooling.

In summary, then, education must afford a chance for every student to experience an individualized, mind-expanding, joy-producing educational process, based on equity of opportunity. But it must do even more. Education must, in the final analysis, address itself to the vital issues of man and his survival. Educators then can take a long step toward preserving life itself.

"Right answers," specialization, standardization, narrow competition, eager acquisition, aggression, detachment from the self. Without them, it has seemed, the social machinery would break down. Do not call the schools cruel or unnatural for furthering what society had demanded. The reason we now need radical reform in education is that society's demands are changing radically. It is quite safe to say that the human characteristics now being inculcated will not work much longer. Already they are not only inappropriate, but destructive. If education continues along the old tack, humanity sooner or later will simply destroy itself (Leonard.)

We must start now.

October 1970

FURTHER READING:

New Careers for the Poor, by Arthur Pearl and Frank Riessman (New York: Free Press, 1965) presents a thorough and insightful description of the rationale and operation of the New Careers program of job creation and training.

Social Relations in a Secondary School, David H. Hargreaves (New York: Humanities Press, 1967) is an excellent comprehensive study of a Secondary Modern School in England which points up the pervasiveness of tracking (they call it streaming) in molding the structure of social relations in the school.

"Delinquency and the Schools," by Walter E. Schafer and Kenneth Polk, in *Task Force Report: Juvenile Delinquency and Youth Crime* (President's Commission on Law Enforcement and Administration of Justice, 1967), is a comprehensive study of the effect of the schools on delinquency.

Rich Man's Qualifications for Poor Man's Jobs

IVAR BERG

It is now a well-known fact that America offers more and more jobs to skilled workers while the increase in unskilled jobs has slowed down. Newspaper articles regularly remind us that we have a shortage of computer programmers, and, at the same time, too many unskilled laborers. The conventional solution is to correct the shortcomings of the labor force by educating more of the unemployed. Apart from its practical difficulties, this solution begs the important question: Are academic credentials important for doing the job—or just for getting it?

My studies of manpower use indicate that although in recent years requirements for many jobs have been upgraded because of technological and other changes, in many cases education requirements have been raised arbitrarily. In short, many employers demand too much education for the jobs they offer.

Education has become the most popular solution to America's social and economic ills. Our faith in education as *the* cure for unemployment partly reflects our inclination as a society to diagnose problems in individualistic terms. Both current and classical economic theories merely reinforce these attitudes; both assume that the labor supply can be significantly changed by investments in education and health. Meanwhile private employers, on the other side of the law of supply and demand, are held to be merely reacting to the imperatives that generate the need for better educated manpower.

Certainly the government cannot force private employers to hire people who have limited educations. Throughout our history and supported by our economic theory, we have limited the government's power to deal with private employers. According to law and the sentiments that support it, the rights of property owners and the protection of their property are essential functions of government, and cannot or should not be tampered with. In received economic doctrine, business stands apart as an independent variable. As such, business activity controls the demand for labor, and the best way the government has to reduce unemployment is by stimulating business growth.

Some of the methods the government uses to do this are direct subsidies, depreciation allowances, zoning regulations, fair-trade laws, tax holidays and credit guarantees. In return for these benefits, governments at all levels ultimately expect more jobs will be generated and more people employed. But when the market for labor does not work out according to theory, when employer demand does not increase to match the number of job seekers, attention shifts to the supply of labor. The educational, emotional, social and even moral shortcomings of those who stand outside the boundaries of the social system have to be eliminated, we are told—and education seems to be the best way of doing it.

Unfortunately, economists and public planners usually assume that the education that employers require for the jobs they offer is altogether beneficial to the firm. Higher education, it is thought, means better performance on the job. A close look at the data, however, shows that here reality does not usually correspond with theory.

In recent years, the number of higher-level jobs has not increased as much as personnel directors lead us to believe. The big increase, rather, has been in middle-level jobs—for high-school graduates and college dropouts. This becomes clear when the percentages of jobs requiring the three different levels of education are compared with the percentages of the labor force that roughly match these categories. The comparison of census data with the U.S. Employment Service's descriptions of 4,000 different jobs also shows that 1) high-education jobs have expanded somewhat faster for men than for women; 2) those jobs in the middle have expanded faster for women than for men; and 3) that highly educated people are employed in jobs that require *less* education than these people actually have.

The fact is that our highly educated people are competing with lesser educated people for the jobs in the middle. In Monroe County, N.Y. (which includes Buffalo), the National Industrial Conference Board has graphically demonstrated this fact. Educational requirements for most jobs, the board has reported, vary with the academic calendar: Thus, requirements rise as the

end of the school year approaches and new graduates
flood the market. Employers whose job openings fall in
the middle category believe that by employing people
with higher-than-necessary educations they are benefit-
ing from the increasing educational achievements of the
work force. Yet the data suggests that there is a
"shortage" of high-school graduates and of people with
post high school educations short of college degrees
while there is a "surplus" of college graduates, especially
females.

The economic and sociological theories that pour out
of university computers have given more and more
support to the idea that we, as a society, have more
options in dealing with the supply side of employment—with the characteristics of the work force—than
with the demand.

These studies try to relate education to higher
salaries; they assume that the income a person earns is a
valid measure of his job performance. The salaries of
better-educated people, however, may not be closely
related to the work they do. Female college graduates
are often employed as secretaries; many teachers and
social workers earn less than plumbers and others who
belong to effective unions. What these rate-of-return
studies lack is productivity data isolated according to
job and the specific person performing the job.

In any event, it is circular reasoning to relate wage
and salary data to educational achievements. Education
is often, after all, the most important criterion for a
person's getting a job in the first place! The argument
that salaries may be used to measure the value of
education and to measure the "value added" to the firm
by employees of different educational backgrounds,
may simply confirm what it sets out to prove. In jobs

for which educational requirements have not been thoughtfully studied, the argument is not an argument at all, but a self-fulfilling prophecy.

Despite the many attempts to relate a person's achievements to the wages he receives, researchers usually find that the traits, aptitudes and educational achievements of workers vary as greatly *within* job categories as they do *between* them. That is, people in job A differ as much from one another as they differ from people in job B. Only a small percentage of the labor force—those in the highest and those in the lowest job levels—are exceptions. And once workers become members of the labor force, personal virtues at even the lower job levels do not account for wage differences— intelligent, well-educated, low-level workers don't necessarily earn more than others at the bottom of the ladder. Marcia Freedman's study of employment patterns for Columbia's Conservation of Human Resources project indicates that, although many rungs of the organizational ladder are linked to differences in pay, these rungs are not closely related to differences in the employees' skills and training.

Educational requirements continue to go up, yet most employers have made no effort to find out whether people with better educations make better workers than people with inferior educations. Using data collected from private firms, the military, the federal civil service, and public-educational systems, and some collected from scratch, I have concentrated on this one basic question.

Business managers, supported by government leaders and academics interested in employment problems, have well-developed ideas about the value of a worker's educational achievement. They assert that with each increment of education—especially those associated with a certificate, diploma or degree—the worker's attitude is better, his trainability is greater, his capacity for adaptation is more developed, and his prospects for promotions are rosier. At the same time, those workers with more modest educations, and especially those who drop out of school, are held to be less intelligent, less adaptable, less self-disciplined, less personable and less articulate.

The findings in my studies do not support these assertions.

A comparison of 4,000 insurance agents in a major company in the Greater New York area showed that an employee's productivity—measured by the dollar value of the policies he sold—did not vary in any systematic way with his years of formal education. In other words, those salesmen with less education brought as much money into the company as their better educated peers. When an employee's experience was taken into account, it was clear that those with *less* education and *more* experience sold the most policies. Thus, even an employer whose success in business depends on the social and psychological intangibles of a customer-client relationship may not benefit from having highly educated employees. Other factors such as the influence of colleagues and family obligations were more significant in explaining the productivity of agents.

In another insurance agency, the job performances of 200 young female clerks were gauged from the number of merit salary increases they had received. Researchers discovered that there were *no* differences in the performance records of these women that could easily be attributed to differences in their educational backgrounds. Once again, focusing on the educational achievements of job applicants actually diverted attention from characteristics that are really relevant to job performance.

At a major weekly news magazine, the variation in educational achievement among over 100 employees was greater than among the insurance clerks. The magazine hired female college graduates, as well as high school graduates, for clerical-secretarial positions. While the employers argued that the girls needed their college degrees to qualify for future editorial jobs, most editorial positions were *not* filled by former secretaries, whether college graduates or not, but by college graduates who directly entered into those positions. And although the personnel director was skeptical of supervisors' evaluations of the secretaries, the supervisors determined the salary increases, and as many selective merit-pay increases were awarded to the lesser-educated secretaries as to the better-educated secretaries.

Executives of a larger well-known chemical company in New York told me that the best technicians in their research laboratory were those with the highest educational achievement. Therefore, in screening job applicants, they gave greater weight to a person's educational background than to his other characteristics. Yet, statistical analysis of relevant data revealed that the rate of turnover in the firm was positively associated with the employees' educational achievement. And a close look at the "reasons for leaving" given by the departing technicians showed that they intended to continue their educations. Furthermore, lesser-educated technicians earned higher performance evaluations than did their better-educated peers. Understandably, the employer was shocked by these findings.

The New York State Department of Labor's 1964 survey of employers suggests that technicians often possess educational achievements far beyond what employers themselves think is ideal for effective performance. Thousands of companies reported their minimal educational requirements to the Labor Department, along with their ideal requirements and the actual educators of the technicians they employed. In many industries and in respect to most types of technicians, the workers were better educated than they were required to be; in 10 out of 16 technical categories they were even better educated than their employers dared hope, exceeding the "ideal" requirements set down by the employers.

Upper- and middle-level employees are not the only ones who are overqualified for their jobs. Nor is the phenomenon only to be observed in metropolitan New York. In a study of eight Mississippi trouser plants, researchers found that the more education an employee had, the less productive she was. Several hundred female operators were paid by "piece work" and their wages therefore were a valid test of workers' productivity. Furthermore this study showed that educational achievement was positively associated with turnover: The better-educated employee was more likely to quit her job.

Education's negative relationship to jobs can be measured not only by the productivity and turnover of personnel, but also by worker satisfaction. It may be argued that dissatisfaction among workers leads to a desirable measure of labor mobility, but the funds a company spends to improve employee morale and make managerial personnel more sensitive to the needs of their subordinates strongly suggest that employers are aware of the harm caused by worker dissatisfaction. Roper Associates once took a representative sample of 3,000 blue-collar workers in 16 industries in all parts of the United States. Among workers in lower-skilled jobs, dissatisfaction was found to increase as their educational achievements increased.

These studies of private firms suggest that many better-educated workers are assigned to jobs requiring low skills and that among the results are high turnover rates, low productivity and worker dissatisfaction. Nonetheless, the disadvantages of "overeducation" are best illustrated by employment practices of public-school systems.

Many school districts, to encourage their teachers to be highly educated, base teachers' salaries upon the number of credits they earn toward higher degrees. However, data from the National Opinion Research Center and the National Science Foundation's 1962 study of 4,000 teachers show that, like employees elsewhere, teachers become restless as their educational achievements rise. Elementary and secondary school teachers who have master's degrees are less likely to stay in their jobs than teachers with bachelor's degrees. And in a similar study done by Columbia Teachers College, it was evident that teachers with master's degrees were likely to have held jobs in more than one school system.

Thus, for school systems to tie pay increases to extra credits seems to be self-defeating. Teachers who earn extra credits apparently feel that their educational achievements reach a point beyond which they are overtrained for their jobs, and they then want to get administrative jobs or leave education for better paying jobs in industry. The school districts are, in a sense, encouraging teachers not to teach. This practice impedes the upgrading of teacher qualifications in another way. Thanks to the extra-credit system, schools of education have a steady supply of students and therefore are under little pressure to furnish better and more relevant courses.

For the most part, though, employers in the public sector do not suffer from problems of unrealistic educational requirements. For a variety of reasons, they do not enjoy favored positions in the labor market and consequently have not been able to raise educational requirements nearly so fast as the private employer has. But for this reason alone, the experiences of government agencies are significant. How well do their employees with low-education backgrounds perform their jobs?

The pressure on the armed forces to make do with "what they get" has forced them to study their experiences with personnel. Their investigations clearly show that a person's educational achievement is not a good clue to his performance. Indeed, general tests developed for technical, military classifications and aptitude tests designed to screen individual candidates for training programs have turned out to be far better indicators of a person's performance.

In a 1948 study of Air Force personnel, high-school graduates were compared with nongraduates in their performance on the Army Classification Tests and on 13 tests that later became part of the Airman Classification Battery. The military's conclusion: "High-school graduates were not uniformly and markedly superior to non-graduates. . . . High-school graduation, unless supplemented by other screening measures such as tests or the careful review of the actual high-school record, does not insure that a basic trainee will be of high potential usefulness to the Air Force."

In 1963, the Air Force studied 4,458 graduates of eight technical courses. Comparing their performances in such courses as Reciprocating Engine Mechanic, Weather Observer, Accounting, and Finance Specialist with the education they received before entering the service, the Air Force found that a high-school diploma only modestly predicted the grades the airmen got in the Air Force courses. In other Air Force studies, aptitude tests were consistently found to correlate well with a person's proficiency and performance, while educational achievement rarely accounted for more than 4 percent of the variations.

These Air Force data do not conclude that education is unimportant, or that formal learning experiences are irrelevant. Rather, it points out the folly of confusing a man's driver's license with his driving ability. Just as different communities have different safety standards, so schools and school systems employ different kinds of teachers and practices. It should surprise no one that a person's credentials, by themselves, predict his performance so poorly.

Army and Navy studies confirm the Air Force findings. When 415 electronic technicians' scores on 17 concrete tasks were analyzed in conjunction with their age, pay grades and education, education was found to be negatively associated with performance. When the Navy updated this study, the outcome was the same. For high performance in repairing complicated electronic testing equipment, experience proved more significant than formal education.

Perhaps the military's most impressive data came from its experiments with "salvage" programs, in which illiterates and men who earn low scores on military classification tests are given remedial training. According to research reports, these efforts have been uniformly successful—as many graduates of these programs develop into useful servicemen as the average, normal members of groups with which they have been regularly compared.

In a 1955 study done for the Navy, educational achievements were not found to be related to the performance of 1,370 recruits who attended "recruit preparatory training" courses. Neither were educational achievements related to the grades the recruits received from their company commanders and their instructors, nor to their success or failure in completing recruit training. In some instances, the low-scoring candidates with modest educational backgrounds performed at higher levels than better-educated men with high General Classification Test scores. The military recently expanded its "salvage" program with Project 100,000, and preliminary results tend to confirm the fact that training on the job is more important than educational credentials.

Military findings also parallel civilian studies of turnover rates. Reenlistment in the Navy is nearly twice as high among those men who have completed fewer than 12 years of school. But reenlistment in the military, of course, is related to the fact that the civilian economy does not particularly favor ex-servicemen who have modest educational achievements.

Wartime employment trends make the same point. During World War II, when demand for labor was high, both public and private employers adapted their recruiting and training to the labor supply. Productivity soared while a wide range of people mastered skills almost entirely without regard to their personal characteristics or previous circumstances. Labor's rapid adjustment on the job was considered surprising; after the war, it was also considered to be expensive. Labor costs, it was argued, had gone up during the war, and unit productivity figures were cited as evidence. These figures, however, may have been misleading. Since the majority of wartime laborers were employed in industries with "cost-plus" contracts—where the government agreed to reimburse the contractor for all costs, plus a certain percentage of profit—such arrangements may have reduced the employer's incentives to control costs. The important lesson from the war period seems to be that people quickly adjust to work requirements once they are on the job.

A 5 percent sample of 180,000 men in the federal civil service shows that while the number of promotions a person gets is associated with his years of education, the link is far from complete. Education has a greater bearing on a person's rank at entry into the civil service than on his prospects for a promotion. Except for grades 11-15, in accounting for the promotion rates of civil servants, length of service and age are far more significant than education. A closer look at one government agency will perhaps clarify these points.

Few organizations in the United States have had to adapt to major technological changes as much as the Federal Aviation Agency has. Responsible among other things for the direction and control of all flights in the United States, it operates the control-tower facilities at all public airports. With the advent of jet-powered flights, the F.A.A. had to handle very quickly the horrendous technical problems posed by faster aircraft and more flights. Since no civilian employer requires the services needed by the F.A.A. in this area, the agency must train its own technicians and control-tower people.

The agency inventively confronted the challenge by hiring and training many new people and promoting those trained personnel it already had. Working with the background data on 507 men—all the air-traffic controllers who had attained grade 14 or above—it would seem that, at this high level, education would surely prove its worth.

Yet in fact these men had received very little formal education, and almost no technical managerial training except for the rigorous on-the-job training given by the F.A.A. itself. Of the 507 men in the sample, 211, or 42 percent, had no education or training beyond high school. An additional 48, or 10 percent, were high-school graduates who had had executive-training courses. Thus, more than half of the men had had no academic training beyond high school. There were, however, no patterns in the differences among the men in grades 13 or 15 with respect to education. That is, education and training were *not* related to the higher grade.

The F.A.A.'s amazing safety record and the honors and awards given to the tower controllers are good indicators of the men's performance. The F.A.A.'s Executive Selection and Inventory System records 21 different kinds of honors or awards. Only one-third of the men have never received any award at all. Half of the 77 percent who have been honored have been honored more than once. And a relatively high percentage of those with no education beyond high school received four or more awards; those with a B.A. degree were least likely to receive these many honors. Other breakdowns of the data confirm that education is not a factor in the daily performance of one of the truly demanding decision-making jobs in America.

The findings reported in these pages raise serious questions about the usefulness of raising educational requirements for jobs. They suggest that the use of formal education as a sovereign screening device for jobs adequately performed by people of lower educational achievements may result in serious costs—high turnover, employee dissatisfactions, and poorer performance. Programs calculated to improve employees' educations probably aim at the wrong targets, while programs calculated to reward better-educated people are likely to miss their targets. It would be more useful to aim at employers' policies and practices that block organizational mobility and seal off entry jobs.

Given the facts that there are more job openings in the middle, and that many people are overqualified for the jobs they do have, policies aimed at upgrading the educational achievements of the low-income population seem at best naïve. It would make better sense to upgrade people in the middle to higher jobs and upgrade those in lower-level jobs to middle positions, providing each group with an education appropriate to their age, needs and ambitions. The competition for lower-level jobs would then be reduced, and large numbers of drop-outs could move into them. (Only after young people, accustomed to a good income, develop middle-class aspirations are they apparently interested in pursuing the balance of their educations.) Current attempts to upgrade the labor supply also seem questionable in light of what psychologists and sociologists have to say. Changing people's attitudes, self-images and achievements is either enormously time-consuming—sometimes requiring half a generation—or it is impossible. At any rate, it is always risky.

If the much-maligned attitudes of low-income Americans were changed without establishing a full-employment economy, we might simply be adding fuel to the smoldering hatreds of the more ambitious, more frustrated groups in our urban ghettos. And if we wish to do something about the supposed shortcomings in the low-income Negro families, it will clearly require changes in those welfare arrangements that now contribute to family dissolution. The point is that rather than concentrate on the supply of labor, we must reconsider our reluctance to alter the demand for labor. We must have more realistic employment requirements.

Unfortunately, attempts to change people through education have been supported by liberal-intellectuals who place great value upon education and look appreciatively upon the economic benefits accruing to better educated Americans. Indeed, one of the few elements of consensus in present-day American politics may well be the reduction of the gap between the conservative and liberal estimate of the worth of education.

Obviously, the myths perpetuated about society's need for highly-educated citizens work to the disadvantage of less-educated people, particularly nonwhites who are handicapped whatever the state of the economy. Information obtained by economist Dale Hiestand of Columbia does not increase one's confidence that educational programs designed to help disadvantaged people over 14 years old will prove dramatically beneficial. Hiestand's studies show that even though the best-educated nonwhites tend to have more job mobility, they are more likely to enter occupations that are vacated by whites than to compete with whites for new jobs. Since the competition for middle-education jobs is already very intense, it will be difficult to leapfrog Negroes into jobs not yet vacated by whites, or into new jobs that whites are likely to monopolize.

Now, nothing in the foregoing analysis should be construed as suggesting that education is a waste of time. Many jobs, as was stated at the outset, have changed, and the need for education undoubtedly grows quite aside from the monetary benefits individuals derive from their educations. But I think it is fundamentally subversive of education and of democratic values not to see that, in relation to jobs, education has its limits.

As the burden of evidence in this chapter suggests, the crucial employment issue is not the "quality of the work force." It is the overall level of employment and the demand for labor in a less than full-employment economy.

March 1969

About the Authors

George W. Albee ("A Revolution in Treatment of the Retarded") is a professor of psychology at Case Western Reserve University. Albee was a past director of the Task Force on Manpower of the Joint Commission on Mental Illness and Health.

Ivar Berg ("Rich Man's Qualifications for Poor Man's Jobs") is Associate Dean of Faculties and a professor at Columbia University. Berg has written or edited numerous publications in the area of business and its administration.

David Buckholdt ("Changing the Game from 'Get the Teacher' to 'Learn' ") is associate director of the Central Midwestern Regional Educational Laboratories. Buckholdt does experiments in the public schools with hyperaggresive and environmentally retarded children in the ghetto.

Donald Bushell ("Changing the Game from 'Get the Teacher' to 'Learn' ") is an assistant professor of sociology at the University of Kansas.

Mihaly Csikszentmihaly ("The Creative Artist as an Explorer") is an author of short stories and essays and translator of fiction and poetry. He is associate professor in the Committee on Human Development and in the College at the University of Chicago.

Desmond Ellis ("Changing the Game from 'Get the Teacher' to 'Learn' ") is an assistant professor of sociology at the University of North Carolina.

Daniel Ferritor ("Changing the Game from 'Get the Teacher' to 'Learn' ") is associate director of the Central Midwestern Regional Educational Laboratories. He conducts experiments with autistic children.

Estelle Fuchs ("How Teachers Learn to Help Children Fail") is a professor in the department of educational foundations, Hunter College of the City University of New York. Recent publications include studies of teachers in city schools, the Danish free schools and American Indians at school.

281

Jacob W. Getzels ("The Creative Artist as an Explorer") is R. Wendell Harrison Distinguished Service Professor in the departments of education and psychology at the University of Chicago. He has published extensively on creative thinking and on organizational behavior.

Robert V. Hamblin ("Changing the Game from 'Get the Teacher' to 'Learn' ") is a professor of sociology and psychology at the University of Arizona. He is completing work on *The Humanization Process: A Social Exchange Analysis of Children's Acculturation Problems* and *Foundations of a New Social Science*.

Jules Henry ("Of Achievement, Hope, and Time in Poverty") authored *Culture Against Man*. He was a professor of anthropology at Washington University.

Jerry Hirsch ("Genetics and Competence: Do Heritability Indices Predict Educability?") is professor of psychology and zoology, University of Illinois, Champaign. He is American editor of *Animal Behaviour*.

John L. Horn ("Intelligence—Why It Grows, Why It Declines") is the author of articles on the development and assessment of personality and intelligence, and abnormal and social psychology. He is professor of psychology at the University of Denver, Denver, Colorado.

J. McVicker Hunt ("The Role of Experience in the Development of Competence") is professor of psychology and of elementary education at the University of Illinois. (For more detail see the cover.)

Carol Olexa ("Programmed for Social Class: Tracking in High School") is a faculty member at Evergreen State College, Olympia, Washington. She is the co-author, with Walter E. Schaefer, of *Tracking and Opportunity*.

Kenneth Polk ("Programmed for Social Class: Tracking in High School") is principal investigator, Marion County (Oregon) Youth Study. Polk is an associate professor of sociology at the University of Oregon.

Ray C. Rist ("The Self-Fulfilling Prophecy in Ghetto Education") is an assistant professor of sociology, Portland State University.

He has publications in urban education, black studies, Canadian public housing, poverty and pornography.

Walter E. Schaefer ("Programmed for Social Class: Tracking in High School") is associate professor of sociology and of the School of Community Service and Public Affairs, University of Oregon.

Karl E. Taeuber ("The Demographic Context of Metropolitan Education") is professor of sociology at the University of Wisconsin. He is co-author of *Negroes in Cities: Residential Segregation and Neighborhood Change.*

Michael A. Wallach ("Creativity and Intelligence in Children") is professor of psychology at Duke University and editor of the *Journal of Personality.* His most recent articles consider the subjects of the talented student and creativity.